NOV 0 4 2009

W9-ANC-783

Viviane Theby

Dog University

A Training Program to Help Develop Advanced Skills With Your Dog

T.F.H. Publications, Inc.

WILLARD LIBRARY, BATTLE CREEK, MI 49017

For Bob Bailey, who taught me the biggest part of what I know about training - at a time, when I thought I already knew almost everything.

Dog University

Project Team
German Editor: Gisela Rau
German Production Design: Marion Luxen
Picture Editing: Thorsten Lukaszczyk

US Editor: Heather Russell-Revesz
US Production Design: Patti Escabi
Cover Design: Mary Ann Kahn

T.F.H. Publications
President/CEO: Glen S. Axelrod
Executive Vice President: Mark E. Johnson
Publisher: Christopher T. Reggio
Production Manager: Kathy Bontz

T.F.H. Publications, Inc.
One TFH Plaza
Third and Union Avenues
Neptune City, NJ 07753

Copyright © 2009 Kynos Verlag Dr. Dieter Fleig GmbH, Germany
Translated from German by Dr. Richard Stephen

All rights reserved. No part of this publication may be reproduced, stored, or transmitted in any form, or by any means electronic, mechanical or otherwise, without written permission from T.F.H. Publications, except where permitted by law. Requests for permission or further information should be directed to the above address.

Printed in China through Printworks Int. Ltd.
09 10 11 12 13 1 3 5 7 9 8 6 4 2

Library of Congress Cataloging-in-Publication Data
Theby, Viviane.
  Dog university : a training program to develop advanced skills with your dog / Viviane Theby.
     p. cm.
  ISBN 978-0-7938-0636-2 (alk. paper)
  1. Dogs—Training. I. Title.
  SF431.T47 2009
  636.7'0835—dc22
                    2009019756

This book has been published with the intent to provide accurate and authoritative information in regard to the subject matter within. While every reasonable precaution has been taken in preparation of this book, the author and publisher expressly disclaim responsibility for any errors, omissions, or adverse effects arising from the use or application of the information contained herein. The techniques and suggestions are used at the reader's discretion and are not to be considered a substitute for veterinary care. If you suspect a medical problem consult your veterinarian.

The Leader in Responsible Animal Care for Over 50 Years!®
www.tfh.com

CONTENTS

Foreword

Don't you love watching a dog learn? You can envision the light bulb turning on above his head. His eyes brighten, the tail wags, and he understands something new.

Many years ago, I had two Shetland Sheepdogs and a three-legged Black Labrador. I bought one of those gumball machines for dogs that you fill with kibble. I thought my Lab might have difficulty with the machine since he was missing one of his front legs, but I was convinced that my smart Shelties would figure out how to operate the machine in no time.

I filled the machine and put it on the floor, much to the excitement of the three dogs. I pushed the bone-shaped lever and kibble spilled out. The dogs bounced for joy and inhaled the kibble. I did this a couple of times, then sat back to see who figured it out first.

It turned out to be a long wait. The dogs just stared at the gumball machine, waiting for direction. For three days, I brought out the toy and repeated the demonstration, only to get the same reaction.

Now, this was many years ago, when I was first starting out as a professional trainer. I trained using punitive methods, since that's the way I was taught. The reason why the Shelties didn't explore and try out new ideas was because in punishment-based training, dogs are reprimanded when they think outside the box. Dogs were not supposed to be creative, they were only supposed to do what they were told. The Shelties were patiently waiting for me to tell them what to do.

My Labrador, Cody, was my transition dog. I had begun attending dog trainer education conferences, and it opened up a whole new world of learning for me, far beyond the instruction in my little community. In meeting other trainers and learning other ways to achieve success with my dogs and the dogs in my classes, I had been inspired to try some "new" ways of training, using food rewards and a clicker. Cody had started his training with the old-fashioned methods, but I had recently started shaping exercises with him using a clicker.

On the fourth day, I demonstrated the machine once again. The Shelties quickly got bored and walked off. After a while, Cody got up, walked over, and pushed the lever down with his nose. Jackpot! The machine spilled kibble. After inhaling the kibble, Cody immediately lay down, put his head on his paws, and stared intently at the machine for 30 minutes, waiting for the miracle to happen again. He had not associated his actions with the results. I watched him the entire time, waiting.

Then, it happened—his light bulb moment. He raised his head, his tail thumped the floor, he got up and nosed the lever again. From that point on, I had to hide the gumball machine from him or he'd empty it every time!

Cody had figured out his actions controlled the machine. The Shelties? They also learned Cody's actions controlled the machine, and that he was always willing to share the kibble! They never did work the gumball machine themselves, they always waited for their brother to do it for them. Which is still smart, isn't it? Watching them learn was a joy, just as it is with my current dogs.

I have always said the day I think I know everything about dog training is the day I should hang up the leash. There is always something new and exciting to learn in this field. One of my favorite things to do is to curl up with a new training book and see what possibilities await within its pages. As a teacher, it is even more thrilling for me when one of my students wants to pursue advanced training with her dog. The reason I offer advanced classes is because my students asked for them, which challenged me to come up with new things for them to learn.

For those of you who enjoy the challenge of learning new things and sharing them with your dogs, this is definitely the book for you. *Dog University* will inspire you to set and reach new goals with your dog. You'll both be learning, but even more importantly, you'll be strengthening your communication skills and your bond of friendship. The best trainers, whether professional or hobby, understand that learning is a lifelong process. Make it fun, and you and your dog will graduate with honors.

—TEOTI ANDERSON, CPDT
Pawsitive Results, LLC (www.getpawsitiveresults.com)
Association of Pet Dog Trainers (APDT), Past President
Author of *Your Outta Control Puppy, Super Simple Guide to Housetraining, Quick and Easy Crate Training,* and *Puppy Care and Training (Terra-Nova series)*

Introduction

Today, great dog trainers are no longer as rare as they used to be. And, as Bob Bailey always says, "The better the trainer, the smarter the dog." The understanding between man and dog is now on such an advanced level that it is a pleasure to watch them work together.

This book is for people who really enjoy training, already know the basics of learning theory, and can incorporate it into their work. It is intended to provide them with new challenges and better communication skills. When our communication is clear, dogs can do things that seem almost miraculous!

The tasks in this book are challenging for dogs. Most are not simple tricks that are quickly trained, and some tasks are meant to challenge the dog's cognitive abilities.

In recent years, scientific interest in canine cognition has become much more intense. In my opinion, we have (until now) reached the limits of our training techniques, rather than the limits of dogs' cognitive abilities. By practicing the exercises in this book you will help develop a dog's cognitive abilities, and you'll be amazed by what a dog is able to do.

The exercises in this book will help you understand dogs better, because they challenge both the dogs and our training techniques, helping them become better developed. Please be patient if you find that it is necessary to repeat the exercises over and over, because you and the dog will both have to develop your skills. This takes time but it is worth it! I cannot promise that every dog will be able to perform all the tasks up to the most difficult stage, but I believe you will learn a lot.

Have fun with your training and discovering just how much dogs are able to do!

Plan your signals

Once you have discovered how fun it is to train your dog, it is useful to write down a plan with all the cues you are going to use. Include both verbal cues and the visual signs you will give with your body. As time goes by, you will be surprised how many there are! The list helps prevent you from mixing up your signals and improves your communication with the dog.

Explanation of Symbols

 **Easy task**

 **Medium task**

 **Hard task**

Chapter 1
Training Basics

General Training Tips

Although I mentioned in the introduction that you need to master basic training skills before using with this book, I want to review some basic training principles because they are so important for success with the following tasks.

Use small steps in your training plan

If you want to train a dog, it is important to work out a plan consisting of many small training steps. You need to have a clear concept of your final goal, understand what the dog already knows that you can use on your way to the goal, and finally know how to get from the starting point to the goal.

I will describe the training steps as precisely as possible in this book. But always remember that there is not one single way to train. There are many possibilities for teaching a certain behavior, and there are also different steps you can take in training. Here, they are presented in one way and as broken down as possible. But you can make each training step even smaller and – depending on the dog's progress – divide them up more and more. The objective should always be to ensure that the dog is successful and getting nearer to the final goal in each session.

Traffic light training

I recommend following the principle of traffic light training. Traffic light training means that you work in small training steps and always in a way that ensures progress. While you are making progress the traffic light is green. If for some reason your training does not progress, the yellow light should start flashing: Attention! You need to find out what's going wrong and why.

If you know what the problem is, continue with your training. If everything works out properly, the traffic light turns green again and you can proceed.

But if you don't know what the problem is, the traffic light changes to red! Stop! Don't continue in this way. You have to change your behavior to change the dog's behavior. Consider where the mistake could be. If you can't figure it out, record the session with a camcorder and talk with other experts about it. But do not go on in training until you have found a way to change your behavior.

Minute training

If you combine traffic light training with minute training, you can make your training even more effective. Training in minutes means exactly that—you train for a minute. Going for *exactly* one minute isn't the most important thing (although this is a good time for most exercises). What is important is that the time is kept short and matches the task. A rule of thumb could be to set the time that allows up to six repetitions of a response. Work with a timer and stop when the time's up. See if you have been more successful in this session than in the session before. If so, the traffic light is now green. If not, you need to go back and figure out what's wrong. You can do 5 to 10 of these short sessions with the dog in a row, depending on the training level of the dog. After that it's time for a longer break.

Training Diary

Between the minute-long training sessions you should keep a training diary. Write down how the minute session went. What was good? What could be done better? What are your criteria for the next minute? A training session ends the moment you plan the next one. A well-written training diary helps make your training more effective. You'll always know which training step comes next, even if you haven't trained for several days.

Also, it helps you avoid mistakes or at least notice them quickly, so you won't drag them along with you when you're training for a longer period.

Never say "No"

Please try not to say "no" during training. This word comes out of our mouths easily, but it is not really helpful. This is extremely important for the tasks in this book, where the challenge is to get the dog to think. Anytime we feel like saying "no" in training, we have failed to show the dog what we really want him to do. And we mustn't punish the dog for our incompetence.

A special signal for "wrong" isn't that helpful either most of the time (with a few exceptions). If the dog really does something wrong, it is best to react in such a manner that reinforcement is minimized—meaning you do nothing—for 2 to 3 seconds (more about this on page 109).

Effective reinforcement

It is always useful to think about how to reinforce the dog's behavior as effectively as possible in training. The reinforcement should not only strengthen the behavior you are actually training, but also make it easier for you both to complete the task. For example: If you want the dog to work quietly, do not reward him by throwing a ball. You can do this in between training sessions as a special surprise if he does something extremely well.

Also consider where the dog is when reinforcement is given. Often it is useful to give your reinforcement when the dog is in a good position to start the next exercise. So we click for action and feed for position.

It is also important to differentiate the types of reinforcement. An excellent effort deserves excellent reinforcement, good performance earns good reinforcement, and so on. If you reinforce everything the same way even though the dog's performance differs, he won't understand what you really want him to learn.

Timing

One of the most important skills in training is good timing. You should be constantly working to improve your own timing skills. Everyone can work on improving their timing! The best way is to practice your timing without your dog. It can be fun if you practice with a human partner. For example, you could click every time your partner touches his left ear with his right index finger. Or your training partner could touch different parts of his head with different fingers. He should begin slowly and get faster and faster to match your skill.

Or you could record a sport like football or tennis. Try to stop the recording whenever the ball makes contact with a person. For example, stop when the a football player catches the ball, or in tennis when the racket touches the ball, and so on.

These are little games that can help you to improve your observational skills and your timing, which will benefit your training.

One thousand possibilities to train

I always say: "There are 1000 possibilities to teach a dog a certain behavior. 500 of them we don't use because they are inhumane, but that still leaves 500 possibilities. The one possibility explained here is not the only one. There are 499 others."

This same holds true for the behaviors in this book. I can't imagine how to train them with any kind of force or violence, because we want dogs who think. You can't make them think by using force. With force you only get subordination.

So my personal hope is that this book will encourage people to use their brains instead of force when training dogs.

Please note:

For the training descriptions that follow it is presumed that you understand the principles of clicker training. It is not absolutely necessary for you to use a clicker, but you must use a marker signal. The marker signal may be a word or a special movement which tells the dog that reinforcement is coming. For some of the  behaviors, marker signals other than the clicker will be not fast enough, so you'll have to adjust.

Teaching Dogs to Understand Words

It is useful for the dog to clearly understand verbal cue words in order to learn the tasks in this book. Obviously the dog will never understand words the same way we do—he can only understand the behavior we teach him. To him, many words will not have the same behavior they have for us. For example, you may teach your dog that "Down" means to lay down. However, when you want him off the couch you might also say, "Down"—but your dog will not understand the difference, and this just leads to confusion. This example demonstrates the importance of making sure the dog will associate the right things when we are training him.

Furthermore, it is important that the dog can perceive the acoustic command, because dogs pay much more attention to our body language than to our words. If he can get his information from our body language, he will not pay attention to our words.

When teaching a dog a verbal cue, he needs to hear the word without seeing any conflicting body signals given at the same time. It's the only way he can understand that the verbal cue matters and be able to learn it.

Example using "Sit":

(1) First say "Sit" without moving your body at all. After a second give the visual signal (for example pointing up with your index finger). Reward the dog as soon as he sits.

 Now wait longer between the word and the hand signal—up to three seconds. Soon the dog will sit before you give the hand signal. Reinforce this immediately.

 Change your body position every time you say "Sit" so the dog learns to pay attention to the word and not your body position.

 Now give the verbal cue while turning away from the dog or when you are standing in another room. Use a mirror to help you to see if the dog responds; or if you are in another room get a helper to tell you if the dog is doing what he is told.

🐾 Important

Give a verbal cue only once. The dog should learn to comply immediately. If you keep repeating the cue in your training, he either won't learn it as a single word, or you will teach him that it is only necessary to respond to the cue after it is repeated several times.

Distinguishing Words

Understanding words are a huge challenge to dogs. They have no problem understanding our body language, but when it comes to words, it takes a lot of practice for them to understand. Imagine if you had to learn a foreign language. Give your dog at least the same amount of time and number of repetitions you would need to learn strange words. And, since your dog's brain is much smaller than yours, it is only fair to give him much more time to learn.

1 Train different behaviors the dog already knows, one at a time, (following the steps on pages 10-11), until he automatically offers the behavior at the verbal cue only. Make sure not to give him hints with your body. The dog should actually listen to the words.

2 Now choose two of the trained behaviors and teach the dog to distinguish the words. If the dog does not remember the meaning of the word in three seconds, help him by giving him the hand signal.

③ When the dog is able to easily distinguish two verbal cues, add a third one. It is very important that the dog understand this behavior on its own, because now we want him to concentrate on the words. For this, he should know the behavior so well that he needs almost no concentration for the behavior itself.

🐾 Important

Constantly change the order in which you give your verbal cues. If you simply alternate regularly between signals ("Sit," "Down," "Sit," "Down") it is possible for the dog to learn simply to change his position without paying any attention to the meaning of the words.

④ Train all the behaviors with a verbal cue, one after the other. Your dog should be able to respond correctly to eight out of ten cues. Otherwise the task is too difficult for him and you should either train the single responses better or reduce the number different signals he has to distinguish.

Brainwork

It is mentally challenging for dogs to distinguish words without the help of visual cues, so this is a good way to tire him out in a short period of time. But you don't want to exhaust him. In the beginning, don't do this exercise for too long, and always end the training session before the dog loses interest in participating.

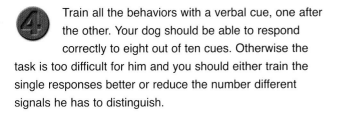

Shaping

As an introduction to shaping, I would like to demonstrate one of the first tasks ever shaped with a dog, if not *the* first task. It was B. F. Skinner who gave a demonstration where he reinforced every movement the dog made to get him to stand up on his hind legs. Try it and count how often you click before the dog stands on his hind legs.

1. Sit down in front of your dog with some good treats and the clicker. Imagine a horizontal line running across the nose of the dog. Always click and reinforce when the dog's nose rises above this line.

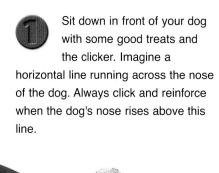

2. Now imagine pushing this line higher and higher. Reward the dog when his nose rises over the line.

3. Next, only click and reinforce when the dog also lifts a paw while trying to lift his nose higher.

Then click and reinforce when both feet are in the air.

 Can you make it clear to the dog that he has to jump in the air completely?

Important

Do not give the dog any help. Try and sit completely still without moving. Only move after the click to give the dog the treat.

Shaping without frustration

Let's take the example of the dog's nose moving higher and higher. Observe how high the dog carries his nose. You'll discover that it is not always at the same point. Imagine that you take ten photos of the position of his nose. The three lowest positions will not be reinforced.

So, in this example, you do not reinforce three times out of ten. After a while the dog will carry his nose higher, so again you will not reinforce the lowest attempts, and so on. The dog will move his nose higher and higher without getting frustrated, because you expect more of the dog when he is already offering the behavior.

However, you can use frustration to shape. When a dog is rewarded for the same behavior several times and suddenly the rewards stop, he will most likely offer more of this behavior because he feels frustrated – and then you can start reinforcing again. But be careful – this kind of training often excites the dog so much that it is no longer possible for him to work calmly. So I prefer to shape in smaller steps, which in the end is faster.

⊕ = Dog's nose above the line: reinforcement

⊖ = Dog's nose under the line: no reinforcement

Target Training

Now let's teach the dog to touch a target with his nose. This is a good basic training exercise to build on for many other behaviors. As a verbal cue for this task you could choose "Touch" or "Target" or whatever you like.

You can easily make a target with a piece of paper glued to a stick. This target will help make it easy to teach the dog new behaviors later.

 Hide the target behind your back after the click. This way you can present it again, keeping the dog's attention and making it easier for you.

Put the target in front of the dog's nose. Most dogs are curious and will approach it. Click exactly at the moment he approaches and reward the dog.

3 Now the dog should not only approach, but actually touch the target to get the click and reinforcement. Again, present the target in a way that the dog can reach it easily. After the click, remove the target and then reinforce the behavior.

4 Now present the target in different positions so that the dog has to bend down, move up, or go right or left to touch the target. When the dog touches the target reliably it is time to introduce the verbal cue.

Important

It doesn't matter what word you choose as a verbal cue. But it should be easy to remember and it should be different from the other verbal cues the dog already knows.

Try to always give the verbal cue in the same tone of voice. This way you make it easier for the dog to understand.

Keep in mind that the dog needs some time to really learn a verbal cue reliably.

Targeting

Target training is an important and widely used training technique. You can choose almost anything as a target. You can also train a dog to touch different targets with different parts of his body.

In addition to shaping, target training is another method of making an animal understand what we want it to do.

Shutting the Door

Now we will use target training to teach a new behavior. Many dogs can open a door by themselves, but this is not a behavior most owners want their dog to know! However, it might be nice if you can tell the dog to shut the door by using his nose to push the door shut. This is preferable to using a paw because there is no risk of the dog scratching the door with his claws.

If the door closes toward the inside of the room and has to be pulled closed, you can teach this with a rope and the pull behavior (see page 30).

 Repeat the target training from pages 16/17, presenting the target right in front of the door so the dog approaches the target and the door. Click and reward the dog as soon as he touches the target.

 Now tape the target to the door. Reinforce the behavior as soon as the dog touches the target. The target is now attached to the door, so it can no longer be removed like the target on the stick. After he gets the reinforcement the dog should approach the target again. Repeat this step until the dog does it reliably.

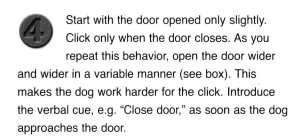

 Then withhold the click for a short moment. Most likely the dog will touch the target more enthusiastically and therefore harder in order to get the click. This makes the door move. Reinforce the harder touches that make the door move. Do not reinforce the soft touches any longer, where the door does not move.

 Start with the door opened only slightly. Click only when the door closes. As you repeat this behavior, open the door wider and wider in a variable manner (see box). This makes the dog work harder for the click. Introduce the verbal cue, e.g. "Close door," as soon as the dog approaches the door.

Cut the target smaller and smaller until it has completely disappeared and the dog does not need this aid any longer.

Important

Always increase the difficulty of a task variably, not in a straight upward curve. In our example, that means that you do not open the door wider and wider for each successive repetition. Otherwise, you could easily demand too much from the dog. On the other hand, if a dog is already able to close a door that's open five feet wide, and is told to close a door that's open only half a foot, he will be motivated because this is very easy. This way you can get the dog to do more and more without him really noticing it.

Not all doors are the same

Dogs learn very context specifically. If a dog has learned to close a certain door, he will not necessarily close other doors. You have to "generalize" this behavior, as we say in trainer talk. This means you have to repeat the training steps with several different doors. Most likely, it will become easier every time until the dog no longer requires any kind of help and has generalized the behavior.

Chapter 2
How Do Dogs Learn?

It's important to take a critical look at what the dog has actually associated during training. Often, the dog has not learned what we think we have taught him. For example, you may think the dog is sitting on the verbal cue only, but you may not realize he's also responding to eye contact. So always consider what else the dog could have associated with a behavior.

Clever Hans

Clever Hans was a horse owned by a retired teacher named Wilhelm von Osten, who lived in Germany at the beginning of the 20th century. Why am I telling a story about a horse in a book on dog training? Because it will demonstrate how careful you should be when training your dog.

Von Osten trained his horse to do mathematics, spelling, and all sorts of things. The horse became famous, and scientists became interested in Clever Hans and came to investigate his intelligence.

In the beginning, they all believed that it must be a fake, but after studying Clever Hans they did not uncover any tricks. In fact, Hans was able to solve mathematical problems when his owner was not even present, so hidden signals were out of the question.

Hans would have probably gone down in history as the smartest horse in the world, but he just *too* good—he could even figure out square roots!

Finally, a student managed to solve the mystery. Oskar Pfungst discovered that Hans always gave the right answer when the person who asked him knew the answer. Without realizing it, the person was giving hints to the horse so he knew how long to paw the ground. Even signals given subconsciously by the audience were enough to tell Hans the answer. However, when the spectators did not know the answer, Hans did not know how long to paw the ground.

For the scientists involved this case was quite embarrassing. They were fooled by a horse! Since that time the "Clever Hans effect" is always taken into consideration when planning a research project.

Just imagine how subtle those signs were, that Hans responded to. The people were certain they were not giving any signals themselves, although in reality they were!

The Clever Hans example should always be a reminder us when working with a dog to critically question whether he has learned what we intended to teach him, or if he is just responding to signals we are not even aware of.

Critical Review

Which Signals are Important to the Dog?

Think about the signals your dog already knows. Critical review means changing different parts of the signal to see whether the dog still understands what you want him to do. For example, when you change the hand signal, the direction you are looking, your position in relation to the dog, the verbal cue, and so on, does you dog still know what to do? Look at the ceiling or move next to or behind the dog when giving a signal. Try to change only one part at a time so that in the end you know which components of the signal are important for the dog. In the photo below you can see the components of a signal that could be meaningful for the dog.

What Did the Dog Associate?

Now that you know what signals are important, you can find out what the dog has associated with the different behaviors. For example, "Sit" means to him "Put your rear end on the ground" if you are standing in front of him and looking at him. If you don't do both of those signals, then the dog doesn't understand what to do.

Now you have an idea what the dog has learned with different behaviors. You can figure out how to modify your training plan to make sure you are making it clear to the dog things like where you are looking don't matter when you ask for a behavior.

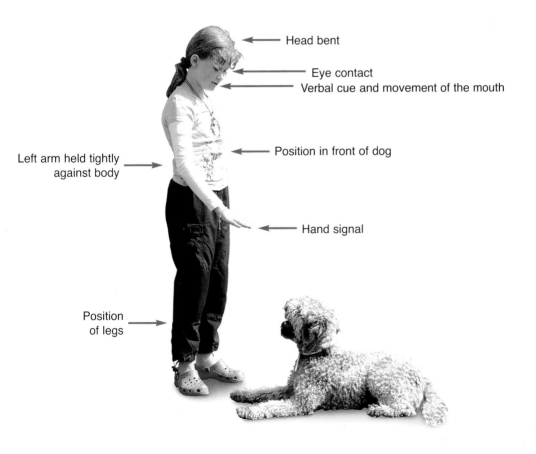

Head bent

Eye contact
Verbal cue and movement of the mouth

Position in front of dog

Left arm held tightly against body

Hand signal

Position of legs

Chapter 3
Differential Reinforcement

Differential Reinforcement I

Many trainers reinforce their dog's behavior in a very similar manner for different responses. For example: teach a dog the verbal cue for "bow." You give him the signal, he does the behavior after two seconds, then: click – reinforcement. He gets the signal again, does the behavior after three seconds: click – reinforcement.

What does the dog learn? That it's just as good to respond after three seconds then after two. The response time, or *"latency"* as trainers call it, does not matter. Is that what we want? No, not really. We have to make it clear to the dog that different behaviors will be reinforced commensurately.

Let's try it:

1 Choose a behavior the dog already knows, either with a visual or verbal cue. Now train him to do it as soon as you give the signal.

Let the dog perform the behavior five times in a row and count how long it takes him to respond to the cue. Reward him every time. Now figure out the average latency. (Example: It took him 2, 1, 2, 3, 2 seconds. The average would be 2.)

2 Choose two different kinds of reinforcers, for example: click – cheese and click – dry kibble. Every time the dog responds in less than 2 seconds, click and reward him with cheese. Every time the dog is slower, the reinforcement should be click and dry kibble. Repeat this reinforcement several times to familiarize yourself with the method.

3 In the next session have the dog repeat the behavior 5 times to determine the average latency. This time it should be shorter than 2 seconds, if your training is still in the green range. Use this new average as the standard for differential reinforcement.

4 Repeat until the dog responds immediately.

Some help for counting seconds

Don't get caught up in counting exact seconds. You're just looking for a method for objectively assessing the dog's performance. One possibility is to count in your head: "one-thousand-one, one-thousand-two, one-thousand-three." The individual syllables provide a fairly accurate time span for estimating the latency.

The average latency you use as a measure for differential reinforcement is only valid for the specific time and the specific training location. It may differ at other times and other places. That's why it is useful to determine a new average every time you start a new training session. You can never be sure a dog who responds within one second during one session will always do this in another session. Every situation is new and it is necessary for the trainer to readjust the criteria accordingly.

Differential Reinforcement II

Now we are going to fine tune our differential reinforcement. To do this, you again work on a response where the dog already understands the signal.

1. Choose three different kinds of reinforcers and a real surprise. For example: click – cheese, click – dry dog food, and just praise, and the surprise can be running together with the dog to a Nylabone chew toy you've placed on the ground.

Get the average time for 5 repetitions.

2. Let's say that the average is 2 seconds (you have counted "one-thousand-one, one-thousand-two"). If the dog responds faster than 2 seconds, he gets: click – cheese. If he is slower, he gets: click – dry dog food. If he takes longer than 3 seconds to respond you only praise him. If he reacts in less than a second he gets the surprise playtime. Repeat this several times.

3. Count the new average and adjust your training accordingly.

Surprise:

The surprise should be something really special for special responses. Decide before you start training which behavior is worth a surprise. Do not give them away too easily. It is not

beneficial to decide in advance "I haven't used the Nylabone yet. I'll use it as reinforcement for the next response." Always ensure that the reinforcement matches the performance.

Now you can communicate with the dog clearly and avoid unintentionally teaching him wrong things by reinforcing different responses in the same manner.

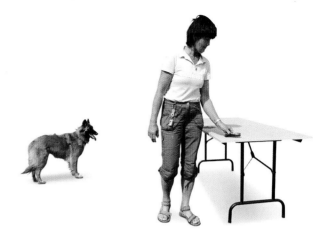

A Trick – Yes and No

In this exercise we're intentionally giving the dog hints with our body to help him (which we would normally avoid in other training). We are taking advantage of the dog's good observational skills and using them to pretend that the dog is able to read. Make two signs, one with "Yes" and one with "No" written on them. Glue them on the end of two sticks. The length of the sticks should be appropriate for the size of the dog. If you are standing upright and holding the sticks to your side the dog should be able to easily reach the signs.

1 Introduce the sign to the dog as a target for the nose. Repeat the target training from page 16. Don't say anything.

2 Now stand upright and point your body directly toward the target. Pay attention to your knee. It should point visibly in the direction you want the dog to go. At first make it simple by using just one target and switching hands, so that the dog is set up for success and gets used to your body language. Repeat this until the dog moves easily to the target regardless of which hand it is in.

3 Now hold both targets in your hands at the same time. Repeat the second step. Give the dog as much help as he needs with your body so that he reliably moves to the correct target.

4. Start to fade out your body signals. Only your knee should tell the dog what you want. With it you should still help your dog answer correctly.

Yes   No

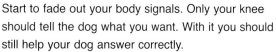

Are humans smarter than dogs?

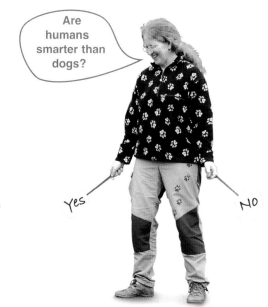

Yes   No

5. Now fade out the help of the knee. By the end, you should only need to tighten the muscle of the leg to give the dog enough information.

6. Ask the dog funny questions and let him answer them with "Yes" or "No," taking care that your audience doesn't notice you are giving subtle signals with your knee. Instead of "Yes" and "No" you can write anything on the signs, depending on what you want him to answer.

Yes   No

Dogs can detect the smallest muscle movements.
In this exercise we use the dog's remarkable ability to notice the slightest muscle movements. Dogs are so much better this than we are that they will recognize movements we would not notice at all. This makes it easy for us to teach this type of trick. Just remember to be careful about not giving unintented helping signals.

Chapter 4
Five Basic Behaviors

In this chapter we will teach the dog basic skills he will need for more sophisticated tasks later on. He will learn to do different tasks such as touching, pushing or pulling something, and retrieving or running around something. If you can, teach your dog all these tasks. Or you can choose only the ones you need as prerequisites for tasks you want to train later. However, to work on your own training skills, you should choose at least two of the exercises in this section to be able to master the last challenge in this chapter – "Putting it all together."

Targeting with the Nose (Touching)

This task teaches generalization. In previous sections, the dog learned to touch the blue target and how to shut the door with this target. Now you can teach him to touch every item you show him with his nose when you give him the signal "Touch." Use objects that are too big for the dog to put in his mouth. This helps avoid mistakes.

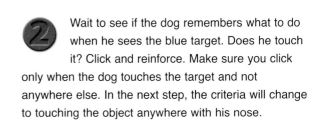

1 Start with a ball. In this first step, you can continue to use the blue target he is already familiar with. Tape it to the ball. Reinforce the dog's curiosity the first two or three times (just like you did during target training on page 16.)

2 Wait to see if the dog remembers what to do when he sees the blue target. Does he touch it? Click and reinforce. Make sure you click only when the dog touches the target and not anywhere else. In the next step, the criteria will change to touching the object anywhere with his nose.

 Introduce your verbal cue "Touch" again. Simultaneously, you can reduce the size of the target until it has disappeared and the dog only touches the ball.

4 Take another item and repeat steps 1 to 3. The dog should understand what you want him to do more quickly, allowing you to reduce the size of the target much faster.

5 Do the same with a third item. Your goal is to be able to present any object to the dog and he will touch it with his nose on cue. See if this works without the target.

6 Test: Show your dog an unfamiliar item, perhaps one so small that he could easily retrieve it. Give him the cue "Touch." Has he understood what you wanted to teach him? If so: Congratulations! Well done! If not, repeat steps 4 and 5 several times with different items before attempting another test later.

🐾 Important

If the dog wants to bite into the item or if he wants to retrieve it, just use a larger item—one that is too big for the dog to do such things.

Another way to avoid biting is better timing. Click when the dog's nose gets close to the item, but *before* the dog opens his mouth, even if the dog does not touch the item. This teaches the dog that his mouth has to be closed during this task.

To ensure that the dog really understands the task, let him also touch smaller items that he could easily pick up in his mouth.

Alternative: Shaping

Shaping is another way to teach the dog to touch something. This is an alternative training method. Simply choose the method you feel most comfortable with.

Pushing

Now you can teach the dog even more behaviors. What else can he do with an object? Let's start with pushing. If you have completed "Shutting the Door" on page 18, pushing was already mentioned.

1 Let the dog touch an item, but without giving him a cue. Reinforce this half a dozen times or until he does it reliably.

2 Now withhold the marker signal (clicks) and reinforcement for a moment. Hopefully, the dog will show you more clearly and energetically that he has touched the item, so that it will start to move. Mark this immediately and reward the dog substantially.

Alternative: Luring

Luring the dog to the item with a treat is another training method you could use. You could, for example, spread some cheese or meat paste on the item. However, luring should be an exception in cases where the communication between human and dog is not quite good enough. In some circumstances there may be no other humane way, thus justifying this method.

5 Generalize this using as many items as possible. When you start with a new item, you will most likely have to repeat each of the training steps. But it will go faster and faster, and eventually you'll be able to present an item and give the dog the cue and he will know what you want him to do.

3 Now wait for more and more movement. Consider the temperament and the learning experience of the dog. You can expect more from a dog who is not so quickly distracted or who already has a considerable amount of learning experience, than from a dog who easily gives up and/or does not have a great range of learning experience.

4 When the dog pushes the item reliably, introduce the verbal cue, which could be "Push" or whatever you like.

Important

In the beginning you can help the dog by using different items for different tasks. This is especially important when training several different tasks at the same time.

An item on wheels is a good introductory item to teach pushing. It moves easily, ensuring quick success and motivating the dog to continue the training.

Different training locations

If you are teaching your dog different tasks at the same time, you can use different training locations to help the dog's memory. For example, you could train "pulling" in the living room with one set of items, while you work on "pushing" in the kitchen with another set of items. This way you can train several tasks at the same time and help the dog remember what he is supposed to do. In time he will generalize the signals so that he is able to perform them in different places. With this kind of help for the dog you keep him in the green training range (see page 8, Traffic Light Training).

Pulling

Now we will teach the dog to pull an item with his mouth. Find something the dog can easily pull, such as an item with a rope fastened to the handle that the dog can hold in his mouth. Or you can just use a rope that you hold in your hand, and fasten the rope to the item to be pulled later. In time the dog will generalize this task and look for a something to pull when you give the signal.

1 Show the dog the rope (with or without a handle) so that he can easily reach it. Click and reinforce any interest the dog shows in the rope.

2 Next, hold off on clicking until the dog's mouth gets closer to the rope, or when he touches the rope, or opens his mouth and takes it.

🐾 Important

Don't take it for granted that the dog will pull a rope fastened to an object as well as he pulls a rope held in your hand. He may associate a rope in your hand with playing, which most likely he will not do with a rope fastened to an object. Moreover, he might be startled when the object moves when he starts pulling. Get the dog used to a moving object before you use it in training, or plan training steps where you hold the rope while it is fastened to the object. Remove your hand when the dog becomes accustomed to pulling the moving object.

3 Then withhold the click until the dog pulls slightly on the rope. When he does reinforce at once. This step is a challenge for your timing. You must click *before* the dog releases the rope, but you need to delay the click long enough to make it clear to the dog that he should pull harder.

When the dog pulls forcefully introduce your verbal cue, for example "Pull." Say the word when the dog starts to take the rope in his mouth.

4 Now fasten the rope to an object. From now on the rope should be fastened to an object, not held in your hand when the dog starts pulling. First reward the dog just for taking the rope in his mouth. After a few repetitions you should encourage the dog to pull more and more.

Shut the door, another variation

Now you can train your dog to pull a door shut. Just fasten the rope to the door handle and let the dog pull. At first you should hold the door to prevent the dog from pinching his paw. After he understands what to do, this won't be necessary.

Retrieving

In addition to pushing and pulling, retrieving is a useful task to train. It is also one of the basic prerequisites for the challenging tasks presented later in this book.

 When the dog touches the object reliably, delay the marker signal (click) for a moment. As soon as the dog opens his mouth, mark it with the clicker and reward the dog. Proceed little by little until the dog takes the object in his mouth.

 For the first training sessions choose an object that the dog can retrieve easily. Follow the same steps for target training on page 16.

When the dog takes the object reliably, have him return it to your hand. From this moment on you only reinforce returning the object to your hand. (You are still right in front of the dog during this training step.)

 Now increase the distance to the dog so that he has to approach you from a continuously increasing distance to give you the object.

Bring

 Introduce the verbal cue, for example "Bring" or "Retrieve," or whatever you like.

 Generalize this exercise with a number of different objects.

🐾 Important

We have now trained several behaviors that start the same way. In each case, it is necessary for the dog to do something different when you delay the marker signal (the click), and he might become confused. You can help him by separating the tasks by location or by time. Separating the tasks by location means practicing pushing in the living room, pulling in the kitchen, and retrieving in the entrance hall. After the dog does what he is supposed to do in the different locations, you can generalize them to the other places.

Separation by time means you begin training with one behavior and start the next one only after the dog has mastered the first exercise.

Go Around (Circle)

This is a good exercise to learn how to use reinforcement to your advantage. We will combine luring and shaping, so that you can see it's not necessary to limit your training to one or the other. You can use whichever works best, or combine both methods for maximum effectiveness. Remember not to "lead the dog around by his nose" when you are luring. While he would eventually learn the behavior with that method, it would take much longer and you would not improve your training skills. What "luring" means in the following text is that your hand holding the treat appears at a certain spot and disappears when the dog has taken the treat.

Your position for this behavior is in front of a cone (or whatever you want the dog to learn to circle). If you imagine that the circle is the face of a clock, you should be standing at 6 o'clock. Remain in this position for the whole training session. The dog should move clockwise.

Click

1. Lure the dog half way around the cone. That means your hand appears at about the 11:55 position, and you feed the dog at the 12 o'clock position. He's likely to take a step in your direction this way. Click this step position and treat at the 7 o'clock position. You lure and feed again at 12 o'clock, click the dog's first step, and so on. Keep practicing until the dog runs easily around the cone. It is wise to first practice your own movements without the dog.

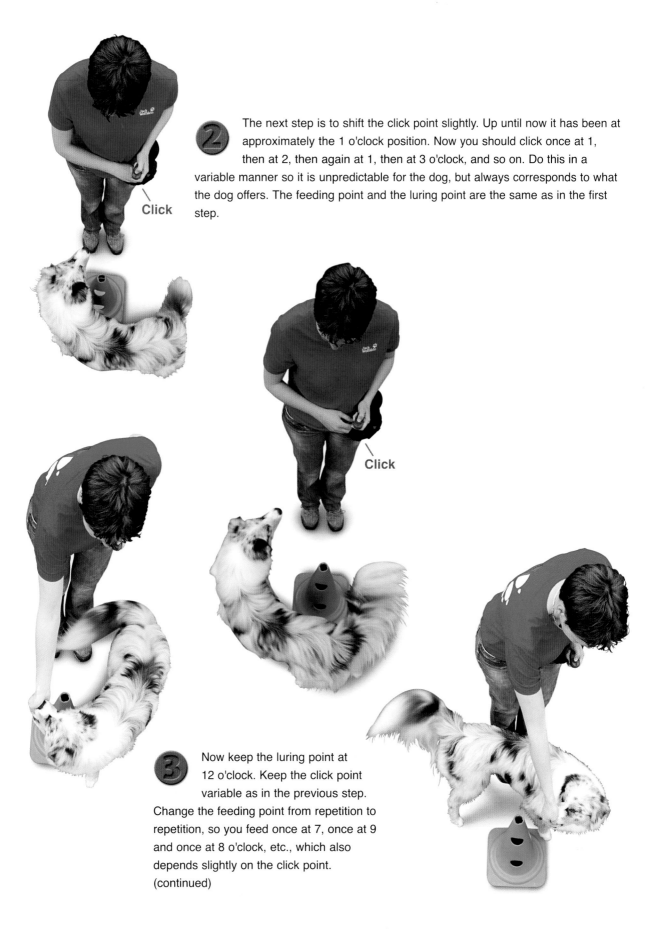

Click

② 2 The next step is to shift the click point slightly. Up until now it has been at approximately the 1 o'clock position. Now you should click once at 1, then at 2, then again at 1, then at 3 o'clock, and so on. Do this in a variable manner so it is unpredictable for the dog, but always corresponds to what the dog offers. The feeding point and the luring point are the same as in the first step.

Click

③ 3 Now keep the luring point at 12 o'clock. Keep the click point variable as in the previous step. Change the feeding point from repetition to repetition, so you feed once at 7, once at 9 and once at 8 o'clock, etc., which also depends slightly on the click point. (continued)

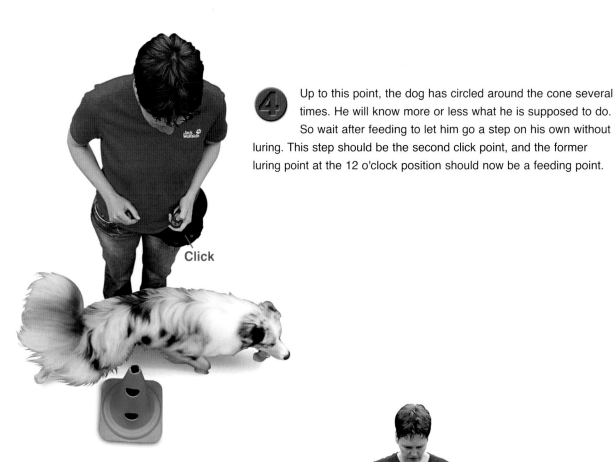

④ Up to this point, the dog has circled around the cone several times. He will know more or less what he is supposed to do. So wait after feeding to let him go a step on his own without luring. This step should be the second click point, and the former luring point at the 12 o'clock position should now be a feeding point.

Click

⑤ Now the second click and feeding point should also be variable, until you can leave out one of the click points with its corresponding feeding point. If you have done it right, the dog will now go around the cone without your help.

If you have mastered this training method, you will be able to train tasks of this type within ten minutes. Otherwise this may take several days.

Circle

6 Now add the verbal cue ("go around," "circle," etc.)

7 Generalize to circle various objects.

Click Point, Feeding Point, Luring Point

The whole purpose of this exercise is to get the dog to perform the tasks at a fluid, rapid speed with whatever help is necessary, but as little as possible. In the case of the luring point it is important for your hand to appear from nowhere and to disappear just as quickly—as soon as you have given the dog his reward. If possible, you should not give any hints with the rest of your body. Have someone observe you or use a camcorder. It is not necessary to click when the dog moves to the luring point. His reward is already there, and the dog has not done anything to deserve a click. During the course of training the luring point is replaced by a feeding point. By this time the dog is already responding without help. However, by selecting an appropriate feeding point you can ensure that the dog's motion remains fluid and he continues to have a sense of achievement.

Working with click points, feeding points, and luring points requires some practice. Nevertheless, it is worthwhile to familiarize yourself with this principle, because it has the advantage of not needing to reduce the aids over long period of time and, in contrast to pure shaping, the behavior is correct from the very start.

Important

It is best to select an object the dog cannot retrieve, push, or pull if you have already practiced these behaviors. Outdoors use a pole stuck in the ground; indoors use a pole stuck in a cone or a chair. This helps avoid mistakes and can give the dog a sense of achievement more quickly. However, you should be able to reach over the object easily to prevent having to move around excessively.

All Together Now

If you've done these exercises in order, your dog can now perform five different behaviors with an object. The dog can now "Touch," "Push," "Pull," "Retrieve," and "Circle." Now we want to test whether the dog really understands the words, or if more training is required.

 Select an item that allows the dog to perform all five behaviors. From the five exercises choose the one the dog performs the worst and refresh it.

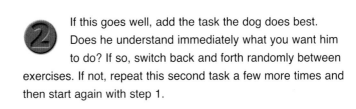 If this goes well, add the task the dog does best. Does he understand immediately what you want him to do? If so, switch back and forth randomly between exercises. If not, repeat this second task a few more times and then start again with step 1.

When the dog differentiates between the two tasks without problems, select another behavior. Again, start with the first training step. Use the behavior the dog does best as the second task and proceed as described in training step 2.

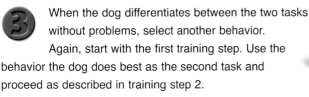

Make sure that you give the dog only the word as a signal without any other help.

 Continue to practice until you have included all exercises.

 Now select the three exercises you want the dog to differentiate.

If this is also successful, have him differentiate four, and then all five tasks.

Important

Please follow the principle of "traffic light training" strictly. With exercises requiring differentiation we generally tend to be rather lax with the training criteria. The dog should already do the right thing 80% of the time, otherwise the yellow caution light comes on! Keep precise entries in your training diary and be consistent. This is the only way to ensure that the dog really understands what you want him to do.

Chapter 5
Advanced Target Training

Target training is a bit more complicated than simply leading the dog around by the nose with a stick. With the aid of a target we can make highly differing tasks clear to the dog. It therefore serves as a good means of communication, and it is an excellent way to get the dog's brain into high gear.

Stationed at a Target

Up to this point the dog has only touched the target briefly with his nose. This behavior was also generalized to include other items. But good target training also includes the dog staying at the target until he is given another signal. This exercise is a challenge particularly when it is trained following the other tasks, because there the dog always had something active to do. Now you simply want him to wait. It is best to practice your timing first without the dog (see p. 9).

1 Go over the simple target exercise again (see p. 16). Use your original target. Pay particular attention to your timing. Ensure that the marker signal (the click) is given precisely at the moment the dog reaches the target. It is better for it to be a little too early than too late, when the dog's nose is already starting to move back. If possible, make a video recording of yourself during training to allow you to evaluate your timing later.

2 If your timing is very good, start to delay the click slightly. Your working with fractions of a second here, because it's too late when the dog starts to move away from the target or starts to do something else, such as biting or pushing it.

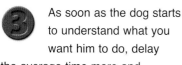

3 As soon as the dog starts to understand what you want him to do, delay the average time more and more. You should work up to ten seconds.

4 Have the dog approach the target from different directions and remain there for various lengths of time.

Practical benefit of this task:

Alternative behavior for when dogs meet other dogs

You may have wondered about the practical benefits of this exercise. This behavior can be very useful if your dog has difficulty when he encounters another dog. If the dog is well trained to the target, have him keep his nose on the target after touching it. This way the dogs won't have eye contact with one another and there will be less chance of a problem. Remember you're asking for a behavior under maximum distraction and that dog will have to be previously trained accordingly. This task with target has a better effect than trying to distract the dog with a tidbit or toy.

"Putting away" the dog when the doorbell rings
Another benefit is that you can station the dog at the target when the doorbell rings. The doorbell can even become the signal for this behavior. Then you can accept a package or let in your visitors in peace without the dog interfering.

Paw Target

Up to now we concentrated on the dog's nose for target training. However, we can use any other part of the dog's body for touching a target. Naturally touching something with his nose is easy for a dog, because he does this frequently anyway. But it is also easy to teach the dog to touch a target with his paw, because dogs also readily use their paws to touch certain things.

1 If possible use a target you have not yet used in training. You can also use your hand for this first step. Put a good treat in your hand. Have the dog sit in front of you. Most dogs try to get at it with their nose first. When this doesn't work, they generally paw at it. Open your hand as soon as the dog starts to lift his paw. The dog will quickly learn that he can open your hand with his paw.

2 When the dog touches your hand reliably with his paw, leave out the treat. Simply hold out your hand in the same way as if you were holding a treat. As soon as the dog's paw touches your hand, give the marker signal (click) and then give the dog the treat.

3 Now add the new target. Hold it in your hand. The dog will touch your hand, as he has already learned. After a few repetitions he will also touch the new target.

4. Now place the target on the ground, on a chair, etc. At first you will need a little patience until the dog figures it out. It may be necessary to use your hand again a few times when the target is in a different location.

Paw

5. Now add the verbal cue that will mean "touch the target with your paw" (such as "paw"). You can now save this special target for this task, or you can generalize the behavior and have the dog touch a number of different targets with his paw on command.

 Important

You need to decide if you want a specific paw or just any paw. It makes no difference which you choose. It is only important to be consistent and keep it the same once you have made a choice.

Light off

The paw target is a good prerequisite for teaching the dog to turn a light on and off. Fasten the paw target to the light switch. At first, reward the dog as soon as he touches the target with his paw. Then reinforce the behavior only when he actually switches the light on or off.

Shoulder Target

Another part of the body that is very useful in dog training is the dog's shoulder. It helps the dog heel correctly. This time we will use a training method that first gets the dog in contact with you.

2 When the dog feels comfortable at your side, start to move closer little by little. Vary the distance so the dog doesn't move away if he has a tendency to be slightly uneasy.

1 Have your dog stand or sit next to you. Reward him a few times if he doesn't already do this and wants to move in front of you. It is okay if the dog is a foot or more away from you.

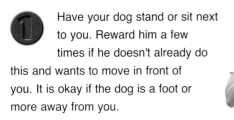

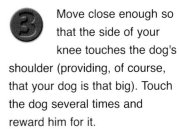

3 Move close enough so that the side of your knee touches the dog's shoulder (providing, of course, that your dog is that big). Touch the dog several times and reward him for it.

4 When your dog is comfortable with this contact and doesn't show any signs of stress, approach him within an inch or two. If he understands the exercise he should move toward you the last few inches, knowing that touching your leg gets a reward. Be patient and let your dog figure this out. Repeat the last few training steps only if the dog is uncertain or easy to frustrate, and appears not to have understood the exercise.

Come close

5 Now continuously increase the distance between you and the dog, so that he has to move farther and farther to touch your leg. Even when the dog can approach from a distance of three feet repeat the task again at a distance of three inches.

6 Start using the corresponding signal. This can be a hand signal or a verbal cue like "Come close," or whatever you prefer.

7 Change the approach angle. Up to now the dog was sitting next to you and only had to move to the side. Now change the angle so that slowly but surely you are standing in front of the dog and he then moves to the right position.

Change distance variably

All tasks involving a distance should be trained variably. The rule is to always increase the distance only to the point that the dog is successful and the traffic light remains green. However, if you proceed in a variable manner within this distance and make the task very easy for the dog once and a while, he will perform the task more and more reliably, because he can never tell what you expect him to do ahead of time.

Simultaneous Multiple Targets: Exercise

Here the dog has to concentrate on at least two parts of his body simultaneously. Our training exercise is to have the dog touch a target in one of your hands with his paw, while he puts his chin in your other hand.

2 Train as you did with the stationary target (p. 38), only this time the dog's paw should remain on the target for a while.

1 Repeat the exercise with the paw target on page 42. Use either the target you used in the exercise or a different one, like a 4" x 4" piece of carpeting. To avoid scratches on your wall, you can fasten a large piece of cardboard to the wall and place the target on top of it. In this exercise the dog is supposed to touch the target on the wall with his paw.

3 Separately from this, train the dog to place his nose in your hand. The palm of your hand becomes the target for the dog's chin. You can teach this either with shaping or by putting your hand beneath the dog's chin a few times and click and reinforce until the dog understands what to do.

4 Practice this so the dog also keeps his chin on the target for a while. Work up to about 5 seconds or longer.

5 Now have the dog touch the target in your hand or on the wall with his paw. As soon as his paw makes contact with the target, give him the signal to lay his chin in your hand. If his paw looses contact with the target, it is not a problem. The dog cannot yet concentrate on both things. As soon as he puts his chin in your hand, click and give him the treat regardless of where his paw is at the moment.

6 Now reinforce only when both parts of the dog's body are on your targets. You have to be very quick in the beginning. Only with time, as the dog gains more and more awareness of his own body, he will be able to concentrate on holding both paw and chin against the respective target.

Here is a variation of this exercise that really requires body control:

Fasten two paw targets to the wall, just a little further apart than the dog's normal "track width." The challenge for the dog is to touch both targets with his two front paws and still put his chin in your hand. This exercise is only for healthy dogs, but is excellent training.

Important

Always make the height of the paw target easy for the dog to stand on his hind legs when he touches it, or if he cannot stand on his hind legs for some reason then easy to get at from a sit. This makes this "mental exercise" good for dogs with hip problems or other physical problems.

Simultaneous Multiple Targets: Practical Applications

A practical application for the exercise with several targets could be used when your dog meets another dog. Have him keep contact between your leg and his shoulder while touching his nose to a target.

1 Have your dog touch the target that tends to be most difficult for him. In the above example, the dog touches your leg with his shoulder (while you are standing). As soon as he does this give him the signal for the nose target as reinforcement. Then you click and treat. Even a short touch is good. Repeat this several times, until you and the dog are familiar with the procedure.

2 Slowly increase the time the dog stays on the target. Always remember to increase the time on the average.

3 Now add motion to the shoulder target. Have the dog touch the shoulder target while you walk. If he makes good contact with your leg, give him the signal for the nose target again as reinforcement and then click and treat. In the beginning it is ok if he he's only doing both for a moment.

 Now increase the time the dog stays against the target while moving.

Now you can add a distraction like another dog, but take it slow. With an extreme distraction like another dog this targeting is difficult.

Important

This exercise clearly shows how positively trained signals themselves act as secondary reinforcement. So be careful and don't use them when the dog has previously demonstrated a behavior you don't want to reinforce. By the way, this also applies for everyday situations, not just for training.

Here Buka is touching three targets. Even though she's 12 years old, she still enjoys tasks requiring coordination.

Specific Activity at a Target

The previous exercise was good preparation for this next task, because the dog did something while touching a target (which was touching another target). Now we want him to do something else while touching a target, such as standing on an object with his front paws while moving around the object with his rear legs.

 First train the dog to accept an object you have selected as a paw target and stand on it. Concentrate on one paw. Naturally the dog can use both paws as it is practical for keeping his balance. But for this training one paw should be in solid contact with the object.

Important

During this exercise you will need to pay particular attention to your timing. The marker signal – preferably a clicker for its speed – must come exactly when the dog moves in the direction you want. Otherwise you could "click the dog to a stop," where he doesn't move at all or he shifts his weight back and forth from one hind leg to the other, knowing that he is supposed to do something with his hind legs, but not knowing what.

Moving hind legs requires body awareness

The more aware your dog is of his body, the easier it is to do this exercise. Some dogs don't realize they can move the rear portion of their body independently of the front part, because they don't normally do this. Usually the hind legs always follow the front legs and don't do anything on their own. Tellington-Touch, working with body bandages, or exercises with hoops and ladders can all help the dog develop awareness of his body.

2 Reinforce even the most minute motion the dog makes with his hind legs while standing on the object with his front paws.

3 Using shaping you can now have the dog circle around the object with his hind legs.

Chapter 6
Signal Control Exercises

Technically, all of the previous tasks were signal control exercises. So are all of the exercises below, but in this section the focus is on analyzing an object.

An Object as Signal

This exercise is intended to teach the dog that in addition to our body language and our words, objects can also be signals. Select an item with which the dog does not yet have any associations, then decide on the behavior you would like the dog to associate with the object.

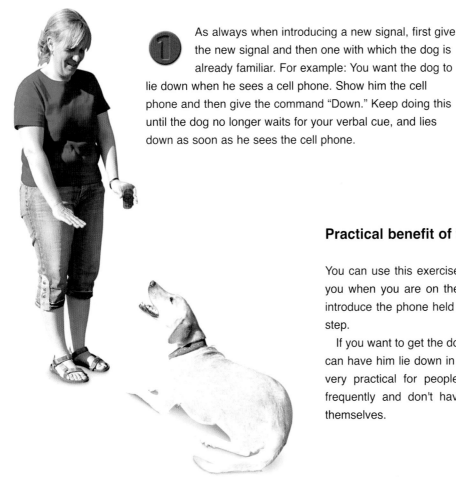

1 As always when introducing a new signal, first give the new signal and then one with which the dog is already familiar. For example: You want the dog to lie down when he sees a cell phone. Show him the cell phone and then give the command "Down." Keep doing this until the dog no longer waits for your verbal cue, and lies down as soon as he sees the cell phone.

Practical benefit of this task:

You can use this exercise to train your dog not to interrupt you when you are on the phone. In this case, you should introduce the phone held to your ear as a separate training step.

If you want to get the dog to help find your cell phone, you can have him lie down in front of it when he finds it. This is very practical for people who misplace their cell phone frequently and don't have it turned on so they can call themselves.

2 Now present the cell phone in a different manner. Up to now you have held the cell phone up in front of the dog. Now place it on a chair, for instance, and approach the chair with the dog. In all probability the dog will not yet know what you expect him to do in this situation. So just give him your signal for "Down" again. Repeat this step until the dog no longer needs your help.

3 Now place the cell phone on the floor. Again approach it with your dog and help him with the signal if he doesn't lie down by himself. Repeat this until he lies down without any help as soon as he gets close to the cell phone.

4 Now change to different locations where the cell phone could be and practice until you no longer have to say anything and the dog automatically lies down whenever he sees the cell phone.

Figure Eight

In the previous example the object was the signal to lie down. The dog lies down and should stay down until you give him another signal. Now we turn to an exercise where the dog moves through a figure eight around two objects. You need to decide if the dog is to complete the figure eight once, or continue moving around it until you give another command. Since the object is the signal and it doesn't go away, I'd suggest that the dog should keep moving around it until you reward him and thereby relieve him from this exercise.

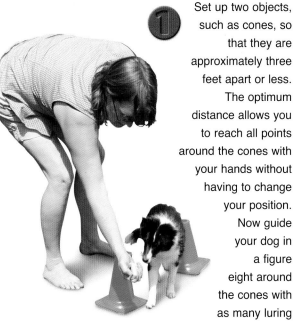

① Set up two objects, such as cones, so that they are approximately three feet apart or less. The optimum distance allows you to reach all points around the cones with your hands without having to change your position. Now guide your dog in a figure eight around the cones with as many luring points as necessary. Remember: You should never "lead your dog around by the nose"; your hand should appear with a treat at certain points and then disappear has soon as the dog has taken the treat. In this manner he should run around the figure eight in a smooth gait.

Click

② Now start to add click points wherever the dog's motion makes them appropriate. The subsequent luring point will then be replaced by a feeding point. Continue to reduce the luring points one after another in this manner.

🐾 Important

Every motion we make is a signal for the dog. We frequently give unconscious signals that are important for him. In this exercise we once again want to practice very consciously not to give any signals. Do not talk and be sure to stand completely still without moving at all.

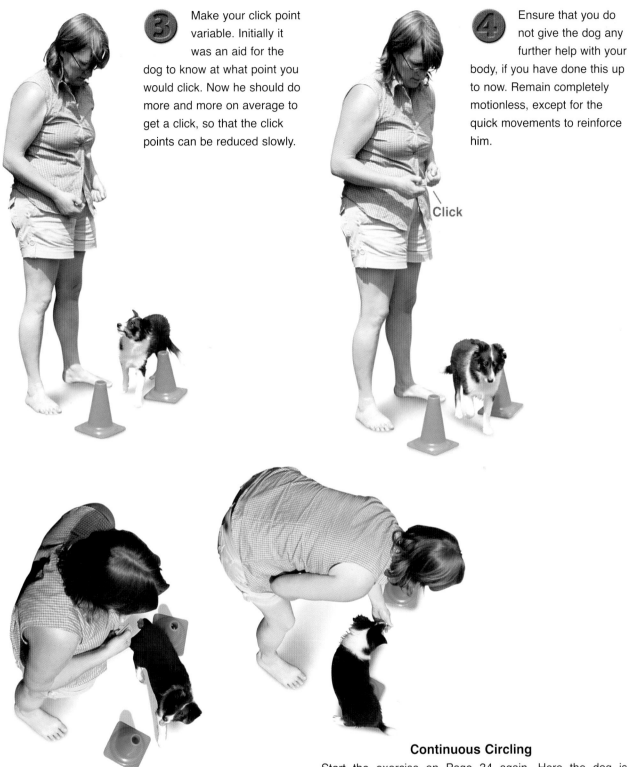

3 Make your click point variable. Initially it was an aid for the dog to know at what point you would click. Now he should do more and more on average to get a click, so that the click points can be reduced slowly.

4 Ensure that you do not give the dog any further help with your body, if you have done this up to now. Remain completely motionless, except for the quick movements to reinforce him.

Click

5 Delay the click points more and more and reinforce at different points each time. Can you get the dog to run through the figure eight six times with only one start signal before reinforcing?

Continuous Circling

Start the exercise on Page 34 again. Here the dog is supposed to circle around an object on your signal. Train this exercise in the same manner as the figure eight, so that you only give the signal once and the dog continues to circle until he is rewarded. Here the training goal could be circling six times.

Figure Eight or Circling

Now we want to familiarize the dog with two objects as signals. For this exercise you need two buckets and two cones (or other objects), and your need to be able to hide one beneath the other. Buckets are ideal, but large flower pots will also work. The dog should already be familiar with the exercises "Circling" and "Figure eight."

1 Repeat the "Circling" exercise as described on page 34, but without using a verbal cue this time. The two cones standing next to one another should be the signal. It may be necessary to give a start signal, but ensure that this signal does not provide any help for the exercise.

3 Practice having the dog circle the cones until you stop the exercise with a click. Be variable with your feeding points and let the dog complete more and more circles on the average. Can you get him to circle six times after giving only one start signal?

2 When the dog walks around the two cones reliably without any help, start moving the cones farther and farther apart. By the end they should be approximately three feet away from one another and the dog should circle them reliably without taking a short cut between them.

x

x

 Also repeat the figure eight exercise (see p. 54) until the dog runs through it six times without extra help.

Important

When you change the objects you need to pay particular attention to your timing! There is only one point where they can be changed so the dog can continue to move smoothly and still have time to react to the new signal (see drawing below).

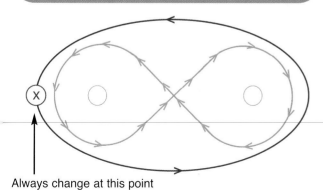

Always change at this point

 When the dog has mastered both exercises, set up the cones for circling. It is best to have a helper hold the buckets for the figure eight, so that she can set them down over the cones quickly. When you give the signal, the helper should place the buckets over the cones, which is the dog's signal for the figure eight. Reward the dog immediately when he reacts correctly.

 Now let the dog start the figure eight. When you give the signal, have your helper remove the buckets. The dog should start circling the cones immediately without hesitating.

As soon as the dog can do both transitions well, have him continue longer on the average before changing the objects.

The training goal could be for the dog to run through two figures of eight, circle twice, and then complete two more figures of eight without any help from you.

Similar Signal and Target

For this exercise, the dog is to touch a target on the wall with his nose. If possible, use a round target with a diameter between 2 and 4 inches that you can easily fasten to the wall. Again it is advantageous to protect the wall with a piece of cardboard. In addition you will need a flashlight or laser pointer with which you can illuminate a small spot on the wall from a distance of approximately three feet. The challenge in this exercise is that the light from the flashlight should be the only signal for the dog to touch the target. The dog should maintain contact as long as the light is on and not touch the target when the light is off. The light spot should be approximately 4 to 8 inches to the side or above the target.

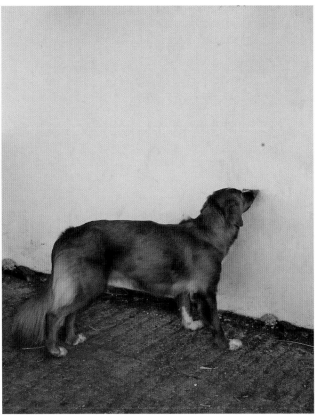

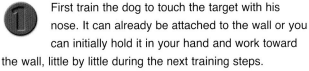

First train the dog to touch the target with his nose. It can already be attached to the wall or you can initially hold it in your hand and work toward the wall, little by little during the next training steps.

As soon as the dog reliably touches the target, introduce the signal—the spot of light from the flashlight or a laser pointer. Move as little as possible at this point. Later, only the light should give the dog the information that he is to touch the target. In this step you make sure that the spot of light is always there when the dog touches the target.

3 Turn the spot of light off one out of five times, on average. If the dog still touches the target, do not reward him. He should slowly begin to get the idea that the light plays an important role in this behavior.

5 The more the dog understands that the spot of light plays a role as a signal, the more important it becomes for him. At some point he will probably touch the spot of light instead of the target. In such cases, turn off the light. Now you have a good opportunity to practice your handling of the clicker and the switch on the flashlight. Don't become exasperated if you get mixed up; allow yourself as much time to practice as you give the dog.

6 After you have overcome the point where the dog wants to touch the spot of light, you can work specifically on signal control. A possible training goal would be for the dog to touch the target within one to five seconds, then wait between one and five seconds and repeat everything three times before being rewarded with a click and a treat.

4 Now increase the number of times without light. If the dog does not touch the target at that moment, you can either click and treat or you can shine the spot on the wall, giving the dog the opportunity to touch the target and thereby earn a reward. If the dog touches the target without the light, do not say "No"; simply wait without moving at all. As soon as he hesitates, give him the light signal again, so that he can touch the target with permission.

🐾 Important

Remember that in this case the spot of light from the flashlight is a secondary reinforcer – just like all positively trained signals. So be careful not to reward any undesired behavior unintentionally when you give the signal.

Commands as Secondary Reinforcers

You have conditioned your dog to the clicker with: "Click – Treat; Click – Treat, etc." He now associates the click with something good. The clicker has become a secondary reinforcer that announces the primary reinforcement.

Now we want to take a closer look at the signals. We trained: "Sit" – Click – Treat; or "Touch" – Click – Treat. So "Sit" and the other commands have frequently been associated with a primary reinforcer. In the final analysis these have also become secondary reinforcers. You can verify this with an experiment similar to that performed by Nicole Murrey and Jesus Rosales-Ruiz at the University of North Texas.

① Select two exercises the dog has already mastered. One of them should have been trained using the positive method exclusively, meaning you should never have even raised your voice to get the dog to do what you wanted. (In our example, it's "Bow.") The other exercise should be one where you have given the signal slightly more aggressively at one time, and may not have been trained with as much attention to the positive method. Maybe you even have a command you used before you started working with positive reinforcement. In our example, it's "Come."

② Lay out two blankets of different types with a little space between. Then start target training. The two blankets are the targets. Instead of a click, give the dog one of the two commands: on one of the blankets one command ("Bow") and on the other blanket the other ("Come"). Then give the dog a reward – just like with the click. Feed the dog so he stands up and can continue without a pause. Do not help—let the dog go to whichever blanket he wants. Give the one command ("Come,") only on the one blanket, and "Bow" on the other. Give both signals in a neutral manner, ensuring that one is not harsher than the other.

Can you guess
which is the "Come" blanket
and which the "Bow" blanket in our
example? Solution on page 143.

Solution on page 143.

🐾 Important

Always remember that positively trained commands are secondary reinforcers. For example, if you always call "Come" to your dog when he's running in the woods, he will start running off into the woods just so you'll call him to "Come," because it's become a secondary reinforcer. If you always call when the dog runs to the middle of the street, the probability increases that this is exactly where he will run. However this applies only when the signal was trained exclusively using positive reinforcement and has not already been "poisoned."

③ Always make this exercise short, about 5 minutes. Observe jot down how often the dog approaches which blanket.

Chapter 7
Training Directions

Now we will consider how to control the dog's motion. In everyday life it can be very beneficial to communicate with our dog in a very precise manner (like shepherds do with their dogs when they are tending sheep). First there are a few basics to work on before moving on to more complicated tasks.

Stand

This training block focuses on precise control of the dog's movements. This helps increase the dog's feeling for his own body and establish the basis for many fascinating tasks. The prerequisite for this exercise is the "Stand" command. The dog should understand that he is to stand still on a certain signal.

1 Lure the dog out of the "Sit" position into the "Stand" position two to three times, and then out of the "Down" position an equal number of times with a treat in your hand. Make sure that you lure him only to the point that he gets up. Preferably he should not take a step.

2 Repeat the same exercises without a treat in your hand. It may be necessary, as an intermediate step, to pretend you have a treat in your hand—but don't be tempted to go back to the first step.

🐾 Important

In all tasks where you lure the dog into a certain position with a treat in front of his nose, the treat should disappear as quickly as possible; after three repetitions at the latest. The dog may not perform the task as quickly then, but don't be tempted to start using the treat again as an aid. First, the dog would be training you, and second, the treat would become a part of the signal you are trying to teach him. When the treat is no longer there and he's not responding, the dog is not being disobedient or stubborn—he simply does not understand the signal anymore, because an important part is missing. Therefore, don't lure too long with the treat; continue to use it as reinforcement.

Stand

3 Now introduce your signal just *before* you lure the dog into position with your hand.

4 Practice "Stand" at many different locations and with continuously increasing distractions.

Forward

From "Stand" you now want to teach the dog to move forward on your signal. Here he should only take one step at a time, so you can control each step. From the very start, decide if "Forward" means "take one step only" or "move forward until I give a stop signal." We will work with shaping, so that the dog becomes aware more quickly that his first step is the important one.

 Have your dog stand in front of you – preferably without any signal. Then move away a little bit. As soon as the dog takes a step toward you, click and reinforce.

Introduce the "Forward" signal fairly quickly. Give the signal just before the dog takes his first step forward. Always click on the first step, because we only want the dog to take one step.

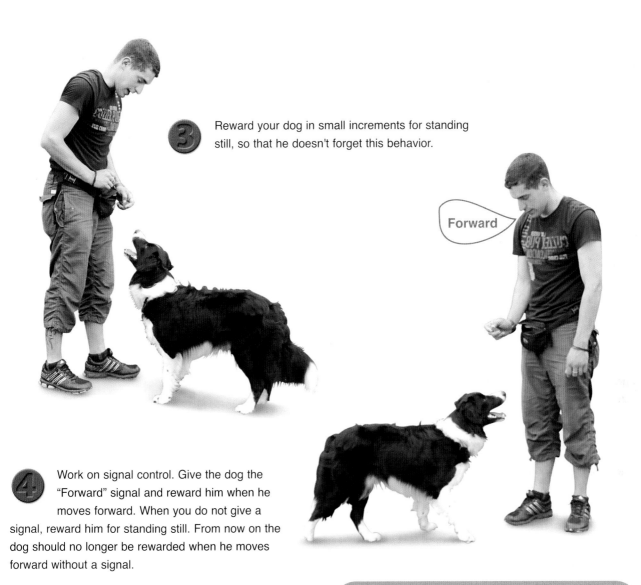

3 Reward your dog in small increments for standing still, so that he doesn't forget this behavior.

Forward

4 Work on signal control. Give the dog the "Forward" signal and reward him when he moves forward. When you do not give a signal, reward him for standing still. From now on the dog should no longer be rewarded when he moves forward without a signal.

5 When the dog understands that "Forward" means: "Take one step forward," start training different numbers of steps before rewarding the dog. But make sure that he takes each step deliberately on your command. It is better to proceed with training steps that are too small than to jump the gun and teach the dog to rush ahead inattentively.

Important

Start this exercise at a specific location that the dog will associate specifically with this task. We want to teach the dog by letting him try things out himself (shaping). However, we don't want to encourage him to do this outside the training situation, so for this exercise choose a special location. This applies for all dogs where "Stand" is used in another context, for example in obedience. As an alternative, you could also use a different signal for this "Stand" in the context of training directions. You don't want to negatively influence tasks that have already been trained.

Back

In principle you can train the "Back" command in the same manner as "Forward"—by using shaping. But here we show another possibility to prove that there is more than one method for teaching a dog a certain behavior.

1 Position yourself in front of your standing dog. Lean back slightly with your upper body to ensure that you do not inadvertently threaten the dog. Now put one foot between the dog's front legs and click as soon as the dog gives even the slightest indication of moving backward.

Back

2 Introduce the signal when you can make the dog move back reliably by taking a step. If the dog is already familiar with backing up from another task (such as dog dancing), use a different signal for this exercise. Here it is preferable to click each step, because in the end you want to control the dog step-by-step.

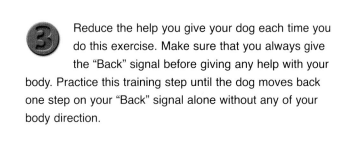

3 Reduce the help you give your dog each time you do this exercise. Make sure that you always give the "Back" signal before giving any help with your body. Practice this training step until the dog moves back one step on your "Back" signal alone without any of your body direction.

4 Start requiring a number of steps backward. Make sure to give the signal for each step and not to reward the dog when he simply moves back without a signal.

5 Finally, the dog should take up to six steps (or more) backward, whereby he should take each step *very intentionally* on signal, with the reinforcement at the very end. Increase the number of steps on the average and check your "traffic light!"

Right/Left

Decide if you want to work with your dog's head or paws for this exercise. In this example, we have chosen the paws. (In the next exercise, "Higher/Lower," we use the head.) However, you can also use the head for training "Right/Left."

Right

 1 Start by sitting in front of your dog and have him put his left paw in your right hand and then his right paw in your left hand (see p. 42).

 2 Introduce the commands for right and left. Give the command just before holding out the corresponding hand toward the dog as an aid.

Left

3 As soon as the dog starts to lift his right paw without waiting for your help, set up one cone at an angle in front of him to the left and another at an angle to the right. In this intermediate step we will use these as paw targets. When you give the command for right the dog should touch the cone to his right with his paw, and on the command for left, the cone on the left.

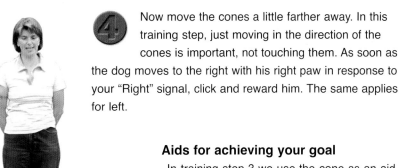

4 Now move the cones a little farther away. In this training step, just moving in the direction of the cones is important, not touching them. As soon as the dog moves to the right with his right paw in response to your "Right" signal, click and reward him. The same applies for left.

Aids for achieving your goal

In training step 3 we use the cone as an aid in the form of a paw target. It may be necessary for you to add appropriate training steps when the dog doesn't immediately understand that he is supposed to touch the cone with his paw. So, you can move your hand closer and closer to the cone, until he has accepted the cone as a target. In training step 4 the cone becomes less important. It serves more or less as a memory aid and will be phased out slowly. This way you can use situations that the dog is already familiar with to make it clearer to him what you want him to do. There is no limit to the number of possible training steps, so use your imagination. Anything that helps the dog is permissable regardless of how absurd an idea may seem at the beginning.

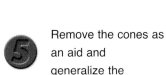

5 Remove the cones as an aid and generalize the behavior at every opportunity. For instance, tell the dog which direction to take at forks in the road or during other exercises such as "Retrieve Right" when there are two objects to be retrieved.

🐾 Important

It is necessary to practice the concept of "Right/Left" in many different contexts for the dog to really understand it. It's essential for you not to mix up right and left, and to remember it's always from the dog's point of view. You must practice this with the dog facing you. Try using a friend as a "test object," to practice keeping the directions straight. It's easy when a dog has a particular marking on one side that you can use as a guide; then, instead of calling the exercise "Right/Left" you can call it "White ear" and "Black ear," if the dog has ears of two different colors. The main thing is not to confuse the dog.

Higher/Lower

This exercise is intended to control the dog's head as the basis for other exciting tasks.

Training goal: The dog lifts his head on the command "Higher" until he receives the next signal. Another goal could be that the dog lifts his head slightly more each time, and the command is repeated until his head is at the right height. "Lower" is the opposite of this.

Again, the commands are only recommendations and can be changed as required. For instance, my dog is already familiar with the command "Lower" in a different context, so I use "Drop." Choose a command and adapt it to the dog's previous signals. The important thing is that the individual signals differ clearly from one another, so the dog won't mix them up.

Control of the dog's head is a prerequisite behavior for tasks that follow. For example, it could be followed by "Touch" or "Retrieve." Our first task is to get the dog to think in terms of moving his head, and then have him do something in this position. This assumes, of course, that the dog already has mastered the commands "Touch" or "Retrieve" perfectly (see p. 26/32).

Training steps for slow and calm dogs:

1 First wait to see whether the dog raises or lowers his head. It is important that you click while the dog's head is in motion and not wait until his head has stopped at the highest or lowest point. Then the dog can be rewarded from a high or low spot. This means if the dog starts to lower his head, click and reward him on the floor; if he starts by lifting his head, click and feed him at a fairly high point that will require him to stretch.

In both cases it is possible to reinforce the motion in the opposite direction immediately. Reward the dog for lifting his head and for lowering it.

Once you have familiarized the dog with this procedure, the next thing to do is introduce the commands. Just *before* the dog starts to lift his head say "Higher," and just *before* he lowers it say "Lower." Always reward the dog each time, and always use the motion immediately after feeding. Repeat this step at least twenty times.

Higher

(This step applies for both show and fast dogs.) Now wait for the dog to return his head to a normal position and give him one of the commands. If the dog understands what to do, click and reward him in the neutral position as well this time. Repeat the two motion directions in random sequence, until the dog does them reliably.

Training steps for fast dogs

With fast dogs you may have difficulty with your timing. It is therefore easier to first limit the exercise to one direction.

Step 1a: Start with the direction the dog offers first and reward him in the opposite direction so you can reward the same behavior again. If the dog lifts his head, click and reward him from a low position, so that you can immediately reward him again when his head moves up. Repeat this until the dog gets the idea of lifting his head.

Step 1b: Introduce the command.

Step 2: Do the same when the dog lowers his head.

Now it is time to introduce the next task. For this we first use touching your hand. This assumes that the dog has already mastered this exercise (see p. 28). Give your dog the signal for "Higher." Instead of clicking, show him your hand at this height and give him the signal for "Touch." Now he has earned a click and reinforcement. (Continued)

The same applies for "Lower." In this step it is important that your hand only moves in precisely when you would otherwise click. The signal that the dog is already familiar with is used here as a secondary reinforcer. Practice this step until eight or nine out of ten attempts are successful.

 Start to delay the command slightly. You now want to teach the dog to wait for your instructions and not do anything on his own. The goal is to make sure that the dog is always successful, otherwise it is preferable to go back one or two training steps.

 Now show both hands to your dog; one above his head and one below. Give the command "Higher" and add the command "Touch" immediately when he lifts his head. Here you have to be very fast with your commands. Be sure to give the command "Higher," before the dog has time to think; otherwise he might touch your hand on his own volition, which should be avoided.

Do the same for "Lower."

 Place two objects to be retrieved on shelves. Place one on a high shelf that the dog can just reach easily and the other on the bottom shelf. Give the dog the appropriate direction command and reward him several times for moving his head in the right direction in this situation.

Now it is necessary to generalize what the dog has learned. Practice at different locations with different tasks.

Possibilities

• Have the dog touch one of three different light switches, and, if possible, switch it on or off.

• Place one item to be retrieved or touched on each shelf and direct the dog specifically to each item.

Sometimes it will be necessary to correct the dog with the opposite signal, because he may have moved up too high. Practice this in small steps to avoid overwhelming your dog.

Always keep the traffic light in mind and stop after two or three unsuccessful attempts. Go back one step or introduce an intermediate step.

 Now, with the dog standing in front of the shelves, give him the signal for "Lower" and then, instead of clicking, the command for "Retrieve." At first, reinforce any behavior that tends toward what you want. He will probably pick up the item after one or two repetitions. This step requires a great deal of sensitivity on your part. You should reward the dog quickly enough to make him feel successful, but delayed enough so he knows he has not yet reached the final goal.

Playing Mail Carrier

This exercise is similar to "Naming Toys" on page 78. However, here the dog is going to people instead of objects, so we need to tell him the direction and control his motion. In addition, he also brings them a message.

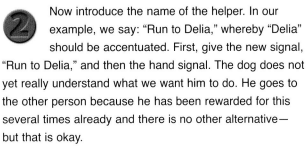

1. First you need a helper to stand or sit at some distance from you and the dog. Send the dog to the helper and reward him when he obeys. He may follow your hand signal. If necessary the helper can also call the dog in the beginning. After a few repetitions the dog should run from you to the other person on a signal.

2. Now introduce the name of the helper. In our example, we say: "Run to Delia," whereby "Delia" should be accentuated. First, give the new signal, "Run to Delia," and then the hand signal. The dog does not yet really understand what we want him to do. He goes to the other person because he has been rewarded for this several times already and there is no other alternative— but that is okay.

3. Have your helper move to a different location. For instance, he or she can go to each room in the house one after another and the dog sent to him/her with the signal "Go to Delia." Make it easy at first and increase the difficulty of the exercise with the number of repetitions.

4 Repeat steps 1 through 3 with a different person. Only this one person should be present, to prevent the dog from making a mistake.

5 Next get two people to help you. They should be positioned a little ways away from you in one room. Send the dog randomly to one or the other helper a number of times. Give him as much help as he needs to perform the task without making a mistake, but be aware of the help you are giving and reduce it during the course of the repetitions, so that at the end you only have to use the name as a signal.

7 You can continue in the same manner to teach the dog the names of any number of people.

6 Then have the helpers go to different rooms. Now you can see if the dog has really associated the names with the people or whether help from you was still involved.

🐾 Important

It will require some effort to get the dog accustomed to carrying a message. You can either have him carry it in his mouth or you can fasten it to his collar. Be careful not to threaten the dog by bending down over him. The two photos to the right clearly illustrate how to properly execute this.

Wrong! The dog feels threatened by someone leaning over him.

Right!

Let's Make a Pizza

This task requires the dog to fetch certain ingredients for a pizza from nine bowls in the correct sequence. This is a good way to test your direction signals. It assumes that the dog is already familiar with "Forward/Back" (see p. 64/66) and "Right/Left" (see p. 68) and "Retrieve" (see page 32). Set up nine bowls or buckets in the following manner:

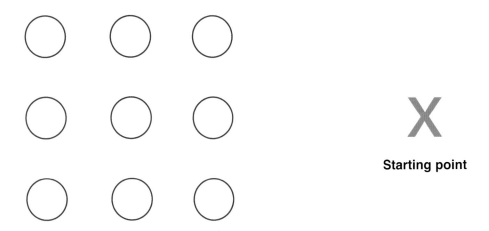

X

Starting point

Now you can send the dog to the bowls in a given sequence with your direction signals to retrieve the ingredients for the pizza.

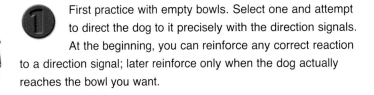

1 First practice with empty bowls. Select one and attempt to direct the dog to it precisely with the direction signals. At the beginning, you can reinforce any correct reaction to a direction signal; later reinforce only when the dog actually reaches the bowl you want.

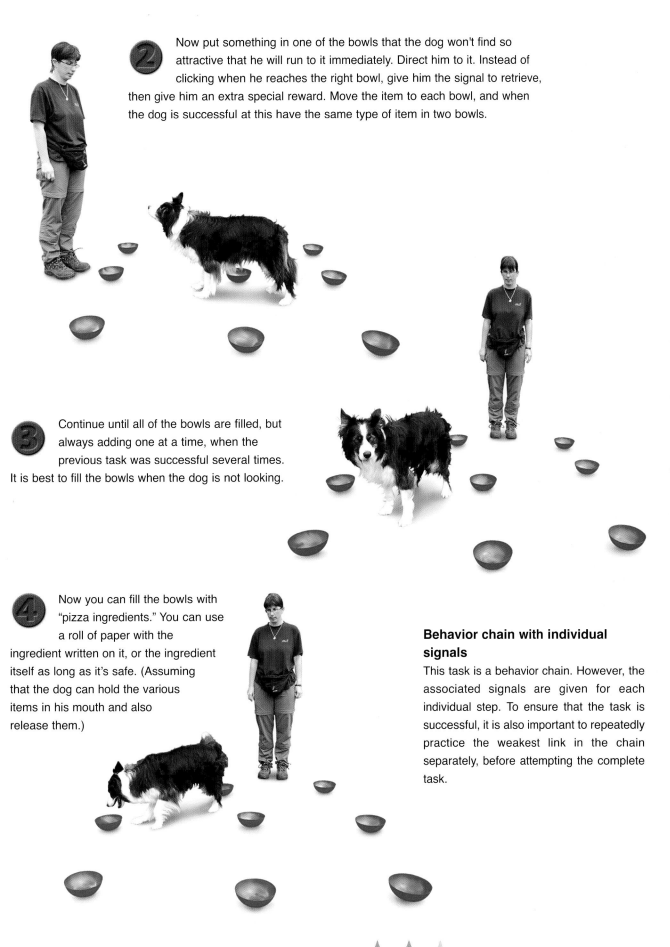

②　Now put something in one of the bowls that the dog won't find so attractive that he will run to it immediately. Direct him to it. Instead of clicking when he reaches the right bowl, give him the signal to retrieve, then give him an extra special reward. Move the item to each bowl, and when the dog is successful at this have the same type of item in two bowls.

③　Continue until all of the bowls are filled, but always adding one at a time, when the previous task was successful several times. It is best to fill the bowls when the dog is not looking.

④　Now you can fill the bowls with "pizza ingredients." You can use a roll of paper with the ingredient written on it, or the ingredient itself as long as it's safe. (Assuming that the dog can hold the various items in his mouth and also release them.)

Behavior chain with individual signals

This task is a behavior chain. However, the associated signals are given for each individual step. To ensure that the task is successful, it is also important to repeatedly practice the weakest link in the chain separately, before attempting the complete task.

Chapter 8
Differentiation

This chapter teaches the dog to distinguish between different things. We begin simply with objects. While distinguishing odors is easier for the dog, it can prove more difficult for the trainer. At the end we will test our dog's visual perception.

Naming Toys

Now that the dog has learned a few verbs, let's teach him a few nouns. Choose one of the verbs the dog knows best to make it easier for him.
   Pick out four (or more) different items that the dog can touch as well as push, pull, and retrieve.

1 Have the dog touch an object that fits in your hand a number of times – as described in target training on page 16.

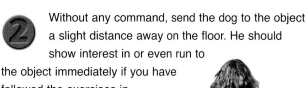

2 Without any command, send the dog to the object a slight distance away on the floor. He should show interest in or even run to the object immediately if you have followed the exercises in sequence. Reinforce this several times. It doesn't matter what the dog does with the item. He may do something with it, but this is not necessary. It is sufficient that he clearly approaches it.

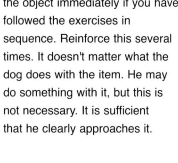

🐾 Important

This tip applies for all exercises: They should always be laid out so the dog will be successful! However, don't expect that everything will always work out perfectly—that would be asking too much. As a rule you can proceed to the next training step when an exercise is 80 % successful. If it is only 60 % successful, the training step was too difficult and you should reduce your requirements a little. This means if only three out of five repetitions are successful, the requirements are too difficult. If four out of five repetitions (preferably five out of five, see box on p. 123) were successful, you can go on to the next training step.

3 Now give the object a name. If you are willing to bet that the dog will go to the item, say the name *before* the dog starts moving. Repeat this at least 15 to 20 times. To keep the dog from losing interest, send him in different directions and practice at different locations.

4 Repeat the first three training steps with the second item. The dog should go to the object reliably even at different locations.

6 Repeat the first five training steps with other objects until the dog reliably goes to the item you name with your verbal cue without any help from you.

5 Now place both objects on the floor at the same time. Set your dog up to succeed. You can either help him by positioning one item significantly closer and sending the dog to it; or you can turn clearly toward one object. Then reduce the help you give little by little.

7 Now combine three objects, and keep setting your dog up for success. Send him to one of the three items, and repeat.

Identifying Odors

Dogs are experts as far as their sense of smell is concerned. Dogs can sniff out things that are unimaginable for us. When we attempt to get the dog to distinguish between various objects or colors in the other tasks, the dog may be relying on his nose a great deal more than we suspect. In this exercise we want to have him specifically differentiate odors. Stainless steel salt shakers work well for this exercise. You can fill them with things that smell, without the dog being able to get at the substance. He can smell it through the holes, but they all look the same.

1 First decide what you want the dog to do after he has found the right odor (like "lie down"). As in the exercise "An object as signal" (see p. 52) it is first necessary to train the signal. So, say you are using chamomile. You'll want the dog to lie down in front of the object filled with chamomile.

 2 When the dog reliably lies down in front of the chamomile container, add another neutral container. Put it farther away at first so that the dog will lie down in front of the chamomile-filled container and not make a mistake. Practice this in different variations.

★ ★ ★

 Slowly reduce the distance between the two containers. Now it is necessary for the dog to really understand that you want him to identify the chamomile odor. He will probably lie down in front of the neutral container at least once. Do not reward him in this case. When he lies down in front of the container with chamomile he should get a special reward. Practice this until the dog identifies the right container eight out of ten times.

Now add a second neutral container. Make sure that you always know which container the chamomile is in—without marking it if possible. Otherwise the dog could rely on his vision, or he could smell the odor of the marking pen and think that is what he is supposed to identify.   (continued)

Continue to add as many neutral containers as you want for this task. Place them far enough apart in a row so that it is clear which one the dog is choosing.

 When you are sure that the dog will identify the correct odor, introduce the verbal cue, something like "Find chamomile." From this time on always give the command before releasing the dog for this task.

Important

Ensure that the neutral containers really are neutral and don't smell like chamomile. Keep the chamomile container separate, preferably in a sealable plastic bag. Do not touch the containers with the same hand—always use your right hand for the chamomile container and your left hand for the others. Then you can be fairly certain not to transfer the odor. Otherwise the dog could get mixed up. The problem is that we can't smell it, so it is necessary for us to be particularly careful with the odor.

 Next you can put various types of tea in the other containers and have the dog smell out the chamomile tea among the various kinds.

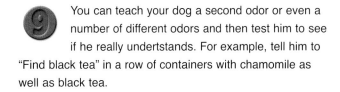 If possbile, work with a helper who can remember the right container in case you forget. In the beginning, the helper can quickly tell you whether the dog is right. Once you are confident in your dog's ability, you can start relying on him instead of a helper.

You can teach your dog a second odor or even a number of different odors and then test him to see if he really undertstands. For example, tell him to "Find black tea" in a row of containers with chamomile as well as black tea.

Find It

Instead of having your dog find individual odors on command, you can teach him to find something you hold in front of his nose as a start signal.

For example, you want the dog to find and identify a certain type of mineral water shown to him from a number of different types of mineral water. (Plastic cups were chosen as containers for this exercise.)

1 Start training the signal with a cup full of mineral water. The dog should lie down when he comes to the cup. (You can build a device for holding the cups, to prevent the dog from knocking them over.)

2 If he goes directly to the cup and lies down, then you can add empty cups as neutral objects. Start with one and increase the number to as many as you like. Add the next cup each time the dog is at least 80 % successful.

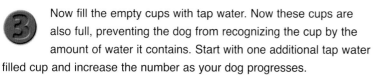

3 Now fill the empty cups with tap water. Now these cups are also full, preventing the dog from recognizing the cup by the amount of water it contains. Start with one additional tap water filled cup and increase the number as your dog progresses.

4. In the next step,
fill the other cups with a different kind of mineral
water that the one you've be training with. This
prevents the dog from identifying the cups by the carbon dioxide in the water that
tickles his nose.

5. Now you can introduce the signal. Hold the cup with the
type of mineral water the dog is to find under his nose
and let him go.

6. Turn your back to the dog when you release him to
prevent giving him any unintentional help. You can
use a mirror to watch him; this will also allow you to
reward him immediately.   (continued)

7 Start delaying the marker signal (the click) more and more. You want the dog to stay down until you reach him. Otherwise the dog might use the click as an aid.

8 Get a helper who can mix up the cups, so you no longer know which one is the right one.

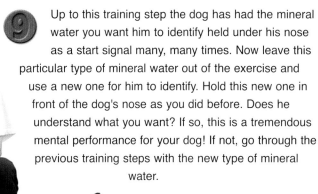

 Up to this training step the dog has had the mineral water you want him to identify held under his nose as a start signal many, many times. Now leave this particular type of mineral water out of the exercise and use a new one for him to identify. Hold this new one in front of the dog's nose as you did before. Does he understand what you want? If so, this is a tremendous mental performance for your dog! If not, go through the previous training steps with the new type of mineral water.

🐾 Important

It's a good idea to use brands of mineral water from different areas, because different brands of water from one area are difficult for the dog to distinguish. Since we don't know exactly what the dog smells, there is no way we can help him. The dog just has to work it out for himself. All we can do is keep the traffic light in mind and select the right training steps.

10 Continue having the dog identify new types of mineral water until he understands that you want him to find the one you show him at the beginning.

 In the final training step place all of the types of mineral water used in training in a row and see if the dog identifies the one you show him.

Distinguishing Colors

This task is intended to teach the dog different colors. It can be used as an exercise by itself or as a building block for various advanced tasks.

Prepare a number of colored sheets of paper or cardboard.

1 Place one of the colors on the floor or blanket (like in "Targeting with the nose" on p. 26). When he goes reliably to this color, introduce the associated signal.

2 Now add a second color. Initially place it far enough away from the color the dog already knows so that you can be fairly certain he will go to the color he knows.

3 In time move the two colors closer and closer together. It is important to vary the location of the paper, so that the dog does not associate the position instead of the color. This means the target color should sometimes be to the right and sometimes to the left of the other color.

 Vary the two colors. Go through various other colors one by one. Always start so that it is very simple for the dog and slowly increase the difficulty.

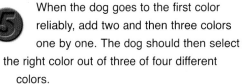 When the dog goes to the first color reliably, add two and then three colors one by one. The dog should then select the right color out of three of four different colors.

 Repeat until the dog can identify three colors on signal.

🐾 Important

Dogs perceive colors differently than we do. They don't have the nerve cells responsible for identifying red. They see red and all mixed colors containing red as shades of gray. This makes it slightly difficult to distinguish colors under certain circumstances. Nevertheless, we can train this exercise. You've just got to realize that the dog will probably learn something other than what you think you are teaching him. When you teach him a ball is red, this does not necessarily mean that he will identify a red block as the same color. But if you recognize these limitations, it is possible to teach a dog to identify colors.

Distinguishing Shapes

Now we want to teach the dog to more precisely visually distinguish shapes. Training-wise, this it is similar to the task "Giving toys a name" (p. 78) or "Distinguishing colors" (p. 88).

Prepare various laminated cards with shapes or foam rubber cut into different shapes. It is important that the only difference between the cards is the shape depicted on them. They need to smell the same, so they should be of the same material.

① Have the dog touch a certain shape, such as a star, several times as a target. (This shape will be called the "target shape.")

② Now place the target shape on the floor a little distance away. If you are sure that the dog will go to it, say the associated command, in this example: "Show me the star."

③ Now place a second shape on the floor a slight distance away from the first. You should make this exercise so easy for the dog that he will go to the target shape with very high probability. Repeat this in different variations, whereby the target shape should always be easier for the dog to reach.

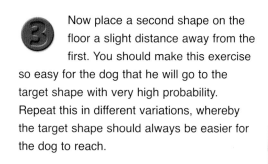

④ Now move the two shapes closer and closer together so that it is necessary for the dog to consciously differentiate them.

5 When the dog chooses the right shape 80 % of the time, you can add a third shape. Continue to vary the positions of the different shapes.

6 Discontinue any aids you may have used. Have someone else observe you or make a video to reveal any hidden aids. For example, you may turning your body toward the target shape, etc.

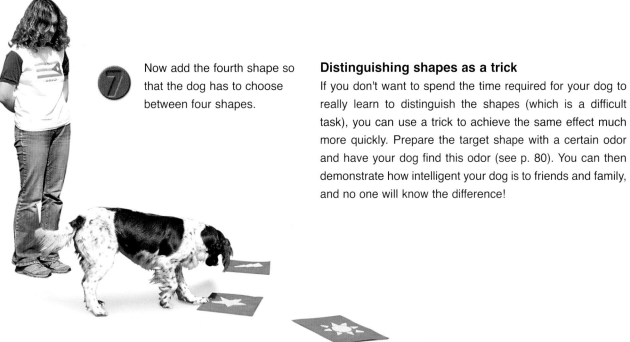

7 Now add the fourth shape so that the dog has to choose between four shapes.

Distinguishing shapes as a trick

If you don't want to spend the time required for your dog to really learn to distinguish the shapes (which is a difficult task), you can use a trick to achieve the same effect much more quickly. Prepare the target shape with a certain odor and have your dog find this odor (see p. 80). You can then demonstrate how intelligent your dog is to friends and family, and no one will know the difference!

Eye Test for Dogs

Now we will test the dog's ability to perceive stationary objects. Dogs are very good at recognizing motion, even at great distances. But what about things that don't move? (This task was also used in a slightly modified form in test laboratories to test the visual acuity of birds.)

For this exercise you need two cards with dimensions of approximately 8" x 8" painted as shown to the right:

1 Select two behaviors, for example "Sit" and "Down." Teach the dog that the left card is the signal for "Sit" (see exercise on p. 52).

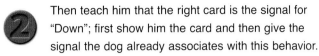

2 Then teach him that the right card is the signal for "Down"; first show him the card and then give the signal the dog already associates with this behavior. Practice these two steps until the dog recognizes the specific card as the signal for the associated behavior.

You can also have your dog use other behaviors he knows such as "Roll over" and "Bow."

3 Practice both at a number of different locations; at first train each one separately.

4 Then take both cards and give the signals in a variable sequence, until the dog differentiates between the cards with certainty.

5 Now you can start the actual eye test. Continuously increase the distance between the cards and the dog. At what distance can the dog still clearly differentiate between the cards?

> ## 🐾 Important
>
> During this exercise, make sure that you do not give the dog any signals other than the cards. At the end of the exercise you might want to place the cards in a stand or hang them on the wall and stand next to the dog to stop any unconscious help from your side.

My Dog Can Count

Let's find out if your dog can count. Prepare two or three cards with dots on them. Teach the dog to touch the card with six dots (as we did with the target in the exercise on page 16). Don't say anything at first. When he touches the card reliably, introduce the command, (e.g. "Where is six?"). Now you can start the exercise.

1 Place the card at different positions on the floor and give the dog the signal "Where is six?", so that he touches the card.

2 Add a second card. Make it easy for the dog at first. Position the card with six dots close to him and the card with one dot further away, so the probability that he will identify the right card is very high. Repeat this several times.

3 Next, position both cards at an equal distance. If the dog identifies the wrong card, take away the right card and don't do anything else. Even if the dog continues to identify the wrong card, don't react. You want to extinguish this behavior. When he stops, place the right card back on the floor and reward the dog when he touches it. Repeat this until the dog reliably touches the card with six dots.

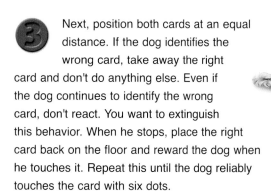

Now introduce the third card in a similar manner. Again, make it easy for the dog at first and place the card slightly out of reach.

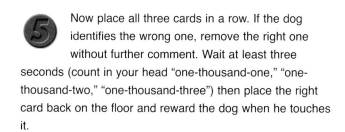 Now place all three cards in a row. If the dog identifies the wrong one, remove the right one without further comment. Wait at least three seconds (count in your head "one-thousand-one," "one-thousand-two," "one-thousand-three") then place the right card back on the floor and reward the dog when he touches it.

Signal check for card with six dots

This little training challenge is intended to make sure that the dog reliably picks the card with six dots, and only this card. Challenge the dog to identify the wrong number. The test is successful if the dog does not let himself be misled.

★ ★ ★   My Dog Can Count   **95**

My Dog Can Read

Task
The dog rolls over when you show him a sign with the words "Roll over" and waves when you show him a sign with "Wave." "Sit" is not as well suited for this task, because when in doubt most dogs sit down when they are uncertain, and you can't tell whether he understands the task or just doesn't know what to do.

1 First practice one of the behaviors. For example, show the dog the "Roll over" sign and give him the command to roll over. Do this until the dog lies down and rolls over when he sees the sign.

2 Do the same with the other behavior. Show him the "Wave" sign and then give the wave signal. Practice this step until the dog waves with only the sign as a signal. Be sure to always present the signs in the same manner, so that the dog does not associate any meaning with the manner in which they are presented.

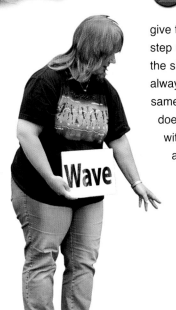

Up to now we have communicated with the dog primarily using words, which is quite a training challenge in comparison to communication using body signals.

But can we teach a dog the difference between written words? Is it possible for a dog to not only differentiate certain words when he hears them, but also to "read"? Of course, a dog cannot read in the same sense we do. He cannot put individual letters together to form words, whose meaning he then understands.

But he can certainly differentiate certain letters or words and learn them as a signal. As with most tasks, the challenge for the trainer is again: How do I say it to my dog?

3 Now change back and forth between the signal signs randomly. First show the sign, then the command to help him. This step requires a great deal of patience. It will take quite a bit of time before the dog learns to differentiate the signals on the basis of the word written on the sign. So be patient.

🐾 Important

During this exercise it is very important to ensure that we do not get a "Clever Hans Effect." Make sure that the only difference between the signals is the word written on the sign. Make a video and observe yourself critically!

4 Delay the command more and more. Differentiate the rewards you give him. Give him a special reward when he does the right thing immediately, and reduce the reward when he needs to be corrected. Keep a training diary so that you can review the percentage of times the dog did the right thing.

Recognizing shapes as intermediate step

Repeat the beginning of the exercise "Distinguishing Shapes" (see p. 90) using the two signs. This may help him understand more quickly that you want him to differentiate between the signs. You could do one session with the "Roll over" sign and have the dog roll over (see "An object as signal" p. 52) and one session with the "Wave" sign where you have the dog lift his paw. Then put the signs back into the exercise "Reading Signs."

Chapter 9
Behavior Chains

A behavior chain consists of a number of tasks performed one after the other. For a true behavior chain you give only one signal at the start. In many of our behavior chains there are enough signals from the surroundings so the dog knows what to do. The tasks then form a logical sequence.

However, we can also invent behavior chains where this is not the case. Such behavior chains provide an excellent opportunity to study and train the dog's memory.

Navigating Obstacles

You can do this exercise outdoors with a few obstacles, perhaps from an agility course. You can also do it inside just as easily, as shown here. Select a few objects as obstacles. For example, the dog can walk or crawl beneath chairs, jump over a broomstick, lay down on boxes, run through a cloth tunnel, etc. The challenge of this task is that the dog is supposed to remember the course himself, so that in the end you give only one start signal and the dog takes all obstacles by himself in the right sequence.

 Work out a course and set up the obstacles accordingly. Now start with the last obstacle. Let your dog do it several times and reward him generously.

 Let your dog practice the individual obstacles alone first. He should be quite familiar with them before you have him run through the whole course.

🐾 Important

Be patient with your dog. Those of you who do agility with your dog know how difficult it is for us humans to memorize an obstacle course – and we have a much larger brain. Wouldn't it be a wonderful training goal to walk through an obstacle course once or twice with your dog and then have him run through it all by himself?

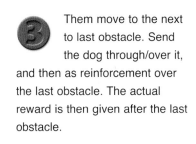

3 Them move to the next to last obstacle. Send the dog through/over it, and then as reinforcement over the last obstacle. The actual reward is then given after the last obstacle.

4 Teach the dog the entire course, obstacle by obstacle in small steps. I emphasize *small* steps, because the obstacles should really be fun for the dog. Otherwise they are not a reinforcement. And, depending on the length of the course, the dog is going to have to overcome quite a few obstacles before he finally gets his reward.

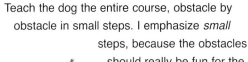

5 Discontinue any aids—for example you may have shown him the direction or run along side of him – so that the dog will finally complete the entire course from his own memory.

6 Set up the obstacle course again differently and teach your dog the new course in the same manner. How long does it take him to memorize the new course? Increase the challenges with a more complicated course layout.

Bring a Drink

This task is a behavior chain consisting of several behaviors associated with each other. The closed cupboard door is the signal for "open the door," the bottle is the signal for "retrieve," and so on.

1. Repeat the retrieve exercise (see page 32). If your dog doesn't know it already, teach him to carry a plastic bottle (without punching holes in it). Begin with an empty bottle. If the dog carries it reliably, fill it with more and more water until the dog can carry a full bottle.

2. Repeat the cues "Push" and "Pull" (see pages 28/30). Then transfer those behaviors to the "dog cupboard door." It is easier for the dog if you attach a rope to the door that he can pull on. Let the dog open and close the door.

 Now teach the dog to take the bottle out of the cupboard. This is different from just picking up something from the ground. The dog needs other skills, so we have to train them.

Now start to put the chain together. The dog should open the door, take out the bottle, close the door with the bottle in his mouth, and then bring it to you.

The next step is for the dog to learn to close the cupboard door with the bottle in his mouth. Be patient. With an object in his mouth the dog perceives his environment differently. It could take a while until the dog is able to close the door without dropping the bottle, although he already does this reliably without the bottle in his mouth.

🐾 Important

Consider carefully whether you really want to train the dog to do certain things. For example, on a long-term basis it could be detrimental to teach your dog to open the fridge and serve himself. That's why for this task we use a special "dog cupboard." Still, there is no guarantee that the dog will not generalize to other cupboards.

To preserve the chain it is important to reinforce the most difficult behavior in the chain frequently. In our example that would most likely be closing the door with the bottle in his mouth. But this depends on the individual dog.

★ ★ ★

Put Toys in a Basket in a Specific Sequence

Like the last exercise, we want to find out how well the dog can remember a sequence. He's learning to memorize. You will need a basket and several objects. This requires that the dog can retrieve (see page 32). The dog should put the objects into the basket in a predetermined sequence. How many objects can the dog remember the right sequence for?

1 Begin with one object. Let the dog put it in your hand, which you are holding over the basket. Reinforce the release.

2 Again, present your hand over the basket, but as soon as the dog releases take your hand away so the object drops into the basket. Again reinforce the release. If you have a cue for retrieving which means "Sit in front of me and put the object into my hand," you definitely don't want to use it here.

★★★

 Start reducing the help with your hand, until the dog gets the idea of putting the items into the basket.

 Now add the second object. Have the dog bring the original object first and then the new item. At the beginning it is okay to encourage him on every object.

 Now you want the dog to pay attention to the sequence. Don't help him any longer and reward him only when he puts the first item into the basket first and then brings the second. You could make it a little easier by placing the objects at various distances apart. Differentiated reinforcement will also help the dog to understand what you want him to do.

Continue to add new items, but only when the dog has mastered the given sequence.

How many objects can your dog remember in the correct order?

★ ★ ★   Put Toys in a Basket in a Specific Sequence **103**

Chapter 10
Advanced Tasks

Now we will test whether dogs are able to understand concepts. I am quite sure that we are more likely to reach the limits of our training skills than the limits of our dogs' cognitive abilities.

On the following pages we present some real challenges. Some of them are taken from scientific research work that was done with other animal species, and some with dogs.

Be Creative

A nice exercise to start with is "101 things to do with a box" invented by Karen Pryor. You reinforce everything the dog does with a box, which could be sniffing at it, touching it with a paw, jumping into it, and so on.

In the following exercise we will test whether the dog can learn to do something new with his body, and whether he can understand the concept of doing something new. Always do this exercise at the same place and preferably on a specific blanket as well, because you do not want the dog to become too creative in everyday life!

① Reward the dog for everything that he does on this special blanket. If he sits give him a reward, if he lays down give him a reward, and so on. He should not get reinforcement for something that he has done exactly the same way before. This means you reinforce each new thing only once during a single training session. In a new training session on another day you can start all over again.

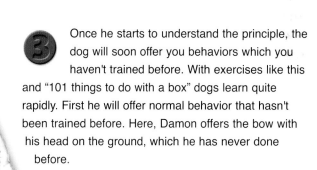

2   With each repetition, develop your observational skills for detecting even minor actions that are new, taking care not to miss anything. For example, lying down on the left and then next time on the right side are two different actions. So are lifting his left or his right paw. The dog will usually begin by offering you everything that was rewarding to him before.

3   Once he starts to understand the principle, the dog will soon offer you behaviors which you haven't trained before. With exercises like this and "101 things to do with a box" dogs learn quite rapidly. First he will offer normal behavior that hasn't been trained before. Here, Damon offers the bow with his head on the ground, which he has never done before.

In 1969, Karen Pryor did a research project where she trained a dolphin to show new behaviors. After thirty sessions the dolphin showed behaviors no one had ever seen in a dolphin before!

4   The next step is the really exciting one. Does the dog understand the concept of this exercise so well that he develops completely new behaviors which do not normally belong to a dog's ethogram?

Two-Part Commands

Would you like to teach your dog to obey entire sentences? First, let's start with commands that have of two parts. This assumes that the dog has learned at least two verbs and two objects or nouns.

For an example, let's take a ball and a cone and the verbs "touch" and "circle."

 Important

Be careful to speak clearly. Leave a clear pause between the two words. Because you certainly know how difficult it is to distinguish where words start and where they stop when someone speaks too fast, even if you understand the language quite well.

 Start training as in the exercise "Naming Toys" (see p. 52), so that the dog reliably differentiates between the ball and cone.

 Independently of this, train the commands "Touch" and "Circle" (see p. 34), preferably with other objects. Train each of these separately until the dog can do them quite well. Then generalize this behavior with different objects.

3 Then put the two exercises together. First take one of the objects, like the ball, and practice having the dog "touch" it and "circle" it until he differentiates the two reliably. When this works, give the command consisting of two words: "Circle ball" or "Touch ball."

4 Do the same with the cone. The ball is now hidden. The objective is to get the dog to differentiate the verbs reliably. As soon as this works with the cone, familiarize the dog again with a two-word command, "circle cone" and "touch cone."   (continued)

5 Next, take both objects and select one of the verbs, like "Circle." Practice "Circle ball" or "Circle pylon" until the dog obeys reliably. Make sure not to give the dog any other help at all, so that he hears only your words.

6 Do the same with "Touch." Both objects are present and you send the dog to one or the other with "Touch ball" or "Touch cone." Give the commands at random so your dog will not be able to detect any specific pattern and has to listen to your words.

7 Set up both objects and vary between "Circle ball," "Touch ball," "Circle cone," and "Touch cone."

The more verbs and/or objects your dog knows, the more elaborate you can make this exercise, making it increasingly difficult. The possibilities for different combinations increase exponentially—with three objects and thee verbs you already have nine possibilities. With four objects and four verbs this number increases to sixteen, etc.

WHAT TO DO WHEN A TASK DOESN'T WORK

The principle of "traffic light training" (see p. 8) is clear: If the dog makes mistakes, we have to make the training steps smaller. However, in some tasks, such as differentiating between things, there is no way to make the steps any smaller. In such cases there is another possibility to help the dog:

Smallest possible reward

The smallest possible reward is a practical method to tell the dog that he is on the wrong trail. The drawing shows where the smallest possible reward is positioned on a motivation scale.

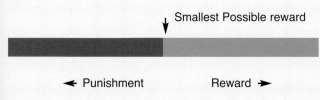

Smallest Possible reward

◄ Punishment   Reward ►

The smallest possible reward to give a dog is simply not reacting to his behavior. Ignoring him would be in the punishment category, just like the signal for "Wrong" (see below). If you react in a friendly manner, something like "That's okay, try again," and perhaps even give him a consoling pat, this would go too far in the reward direction. And that is not what we want to do when his behavior was wrong. So the best thing to do is not to react at all for three seconds, as if you didn't even notice his behavior. With repetition the dog learns to use this information as an aid.

Ensuring Failure

In some tasks the dog exhibits a behavior that is so rewarding for himself that he no longer cares about getting a reward from us. Or the behavior is so "easy" that he simply tries one thing after another until he does the right thing by chance. For example, knocking over the blocks in "The Concept of Middle" was so much fun for Damon that he simply kept trying until he got to the right block. Unfortunately this prevented any further progress. The solution was to hold the wrong block in place, so he couldn't knock it over. This made the dog "think" and his behavior was correct much more frequently. However, it is necessary not to provide too much help, because it's hard to reduce later; otherwise the dog quickly learns: "Knock over the block that isn't being held." And that isn't what we want.

Removing the Possibility of a Reward

If, for instance, when distinguishing shapes (see p. 90) the dog picks the star and still doesn't understand the exercise after a number of repetitions, a possibility is to remove the star when he identifies the wrong shape. This is a form of punishment, because you take away the possibility of earning a reward. Precise timing is important here: The correct shape should disappear exactly at the moment the dog chooses the wrong shape. It should then remain hidden until the incorrect behavior is cancelled, in the best case scenario. Then, and only then, should the star be returned. Exact timing is also required here, because returning the star is like a secondary reinforcer. It is necessary for you to also pay particular attention to reinforcing the desired behavior. This process can be very frustrating for your dog. However, in some cases it can be an aid so that your training continues to progress, because some errors are so rewarding for the dog that you cannot achieve anything by resorting to the smallest possible reward.

"Wrong" Signal

A well practiced "Wrong" signal can be a valuable aid for the dog. It means that a certain behavior does not deserve a reward. If the dog makes a mistake, he gets a certain signal such as "unh-unh" and then no treat. It is important to give this signal with as little emotion as possible. It is not intended as a punishment in the conventional sense. However, withholding a reward is a form of punishment. The "wrong" signal is a conditioned punishment signal, just as the clicker is a conditioned reinforcer. It should be used carefully, because it could result in stress for sensitive dogs. Be attentive and consider whether it is appropriate. In some cases it may be an invaluable aid in helping the dog understand the task.

Caution!

With the exception of the smallest possible reward, these techniques are all punishments. Used cautiously and deliberately, they can be a valuable possibility for communicating with the dog. But it is necessary to be very careful not to punish the dog for your own shortcomings as a trainer.

Three-Part Commands

You can try this exercise after you have already taught your dog a number of verbs (touch, circle, retrieve, etc.), a number of nouns (cube, ball, cone, etc.) and a number of adjectives (various colors). For this task you need at least two different objects, each in two colors (in our example a blue and green cube and a blue and green bowl).

1 Refresh all of the cue words individually (see corresponding exercises).

2 Start combining two commands. Go through the various possibilities. So for our example, we used: "Touch cube," "Circle cube," "Touch dish," "Circle dish." For this step, lay out only one of each type of object (see also "Two-part Commands" p. 106).

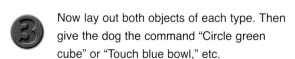

 Now lay out both objects of each type. Then give the dog the command "Circle green cube" or "Touch blue bowl," etc.

Depending on the dog's ability you can add objects, colors and, of course, things to do with each of them.

Important

Consider the sequence in which you say the words.

Dogs do not have our sense of word order. The sequence makes no difference to them, but the dog does have to wait until all of the words in the command have been spoken. This could present problems, particularly with quick, eager dogs. Therefore it might be preferable to say the verb last as the start signal for the exercise. You could also use a random word sequence and use a body cue as the start signal. Again the important thing is to consider critically – particularly if the dog makes mistakes – if it is possible for him to understand what we want him to do at all, and if there is any other way to make it clear to him.

Bring an Identical Object

For this exercise you need two identical sets of three dog toys. Your dog should have a clear preference between the toys. One of them should be his absolute favorite toy (Toy 1), the second toy less popular (Toy 2), and the third toy one he likes even less (Toy 3). Initially always use the same location for this exercise (up to Step 6). Have the dog sit down in front of you so that he associates this location and his behavior with this exercise.

The title says "Bring" an identical object. However, if your dog cannot retrieve, you can perform this exercise with another behavior. For example, the dog could touch the object with his paw or lay down in front of it, etc. There are no limits to your creativity here.

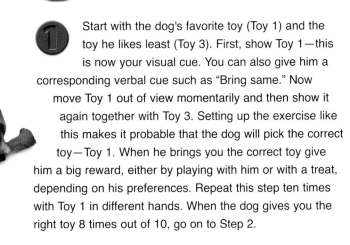

1 Start with the dog's favorite toy (Toy 1) and the toy he likes least (Toy 3). First, show Toy 1—this is now your visual cue. You can also give him a corresponding verbal cue such as "Bring same." Now move Toy 1 out of view momentarily and then show it again together with Toy 3. Setting up the exercise like this makes it probable that the dog will pick the correct toy—Toy 1. When he brings you the correct toy give him a big reward, either by playing with him or with a treat, depending on his preferences. Repeat this step ten times with Toy 1 in different hands. When the dog gives you the right toy 8 times out of 10, go on to Step 2.

Repeat Step 1 with the toy that is your dog's second favorite (Toy 2). Show him Toy 2 as the signal and give the verbal cue. Then show him Toy 2 together with Toy 3. The dog will most likely choose the right toy here as well. Repeat this step ten times, randomly changing the hand in which you hold Toy 2. This means you should not simply change back and forth from your right hand to your left. The dog could quickly learn this pattern. Instead, you should change randomly. For example: right, left, left, right, right, left, right, right, left, left, etc. When the dog gives you the correct toy at least 8 out of 10 times, continue with Step 3.

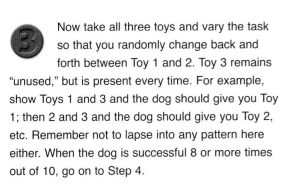

Now take all three toys and vary the task so that you randomly change back and forth between Toy 1 and 2. Toy 3 remains "unused," but is present every time. For example, show Toys 1 and 3 and the dog should give you Toy 1; then 2 and 3 and the dog should give you Toy 2, etc. Remember not to lapse into any pattern here either. When the dog is successful 8 or more times out of 10, go on to Step 4.

Now take Toys 1 and 2. First have your dog select Toy 1. The next time, show him Toy 2, which is the one he needs to choose. This is a very decisive step. You'll see for the first time whether the dog has understood the exercise. Up to this point the exercises were laid out so the dog would, in all probability, select the right toy (because it was always the favored toy). Now you can check whether he understands that you showing him the toy is the preliminary signal for selecting the toy. If he picks the right toy this time, you have hit the jackpot! Celebrate with the dog. Repeat this exercise ten times, alternately presenting the dog Toy 1 and Toy 2. When he is successful 8 times out of 10 proceed to Step 5.   (Continued)

Now take all three toys and have the dog pick one of them randomly. Once again we come to a crucial step, as you will show him Toy 3, and up to this time he has not had to choose this toy. It's further proof of whether he has really understood the concept and picks Toy 3 instead of his favorite toy. If he does you have hit the jackpot again! Repeat this step ten times, varying between the three toys at random. When he picks the right toy 8 out of 10 times, continue with the next step.

Up to now you have worked with only one set of toys to ensure that your dog was successful. Now we will start using the second set of identical toys. Have your dog sit in front of you at the usual location. However, this time place the three toys on the floor in front of him. Now present him with one of the toys (for example, Toy 2) and the dog should pick the same Toy 2 from those lying on the floor in front of him. When he picks the right one 8 or more times out of 10 proceed with the next step.

7 Now the challenge is to train this behavior at different locations. Practice it once in the kitchen, then in the yard. Continue to have your dog sit down at the beginning of the exercise, so that he will recognize the ritual and know what is going to happen. Repeat steps 1 to 6 at the various locations.

8 Instead of using the familiar toys, start including other objects. The new objects should also be in pairs—one for use as a signal and the other for the dog to pick out. First, include one new object in the existing set of toys. If your dogs picks the new object correctly after you have presented it, you have once again hit the jackpot!

Note:
It is not possible for us to say what "the same" means for a dog. Does he depend more on the appearance or the smell? Probably the latter, so it is necessary to handle the objects in the same manner. You should touch them, pick them up in your hand, etc. approximately the same number of times and wash them together. Otherwise what seems to be the "same" to us, could differ quite a bit for the dog, because the odor is different.

Bring an identical object using a specific path
If you have already taught the dog right and left you can make this exercise even more demanding. You need 3 identical sets of toys. Place one pile of toys at some distance to the right and another at the same distance to the left. Then send him either to the left or right with the appropriate command to pick the same object out of that pile. Make sure that the dog doesn't have any help other than your spoken word, if you really want to test his mental ability and your training competency. Another possibility is to teach the dog the objects such as "box," "basket" or perhaps "chair" or other places, which is usually simpler than the concept of left and right. Then the toys from which the dog is to pick are located in a box or on a chair. You give the dog the signal for "Bring same" and then the additional location where the items are located.

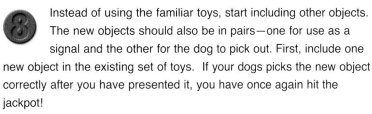

The Concept of "Middle"

This task places enormous demands on the cognitive abilities of your dog. This type of exercise has been performed with monkeys to study whether they could understand the concept of "middle." Now we want to see whether you can also get your dog to understand this concept: His task is to always bring, touch, or knock over the object located in the middle of a row consisting of an uneven number of objects. These can be whatever you want; in this example we use blocks, and the dog knocks over the one in the middle.

1 It is first necessary to first teach the dog to knock over one block. Try this with the "Touch" signal. The block may fall over when he touches it. Or give the dog the signal for "Push"; then it is certain to fall over.

2 When the dog can knock the block over reliably, position other blocks to the left and right of the first. Continue to reward the dog for knocking over the familiar block. He still does not understand what "middle" is, he just keeps doing what he has done the whole time.

3 Now move these three blocks all slightly to the side. The dog will now knock over either the middle block, because he has gotten used to it, or he will select the block now located at the position of the first block he has knocked over the whole time, because he has become accustomed to the location. In the latter case you will have to make it clear to him that he only gets a reward for the middle block. Do this at a number of different locations.

4 Now select a block other than the middle one (i.e., not the one the dog has been knocking over the whole time). Preferably take this block completely out of the exercise for a while. If the dog does not understand what you want, start over again with the first training step using the new block. Continue this sequence of training steps using new blocks until the dog always knocks over the one in the middle, regardless of which block you use and at which position they are located. (continued)

5 Now you can check whether the dog still understands the task when two more blocks are located to the left and right of the middle block. We now have five blocks in the row. At first, use a different color for the two outermost blocks so that the difference is clear to the dog and he can continue to pick the middle from the combination of three blocks familiar to him. When he knocks over the middle block reliably, use five blocks of the same color. Can he do this as well?

★ ★ ★

Continue to add blocks in this manner and see if your dog can find the middle with seven blocks or with nine blocks, etc.

🐾 Important

During this task it is extremely important to consider the "Clever Hans effect" (see p. 20). Continue to make sure that you do not give the dog any unintentional signals he could use as an aid in solving the problem. Does he really understand the concept? Always remember to scrutinize critically (see p. 21).

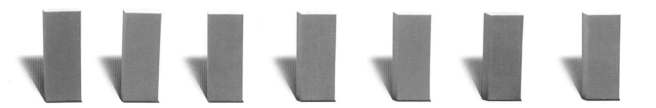

★ ★ ★

Which is Biggest?

Can a dog understand a concept like this? Actually, the real question is: Are we capable of making it clear to the dog what we really want? Image the dog has his choice between a small bone and a large one. It is fairly certain he will pick the large one because he already an understanding of "more." But how can we make it clear to him that this is the choice we want him to make? For this task you need three or four of exactly the same object that differ only in terms of size.

1 Decide how you want the dog to indicate the biggest object. Do you want him to retrieve it, lie down in front of it, or simply touch the right one? In this example we have chosen "retrieve." Refresh the dog's retrieve by having him retrieve the largest object.

2 Now show the dog the largest item and a significantly smaller one (the smallest of three) for selection. First place the smaller object a little farther away from the dog to prevent errors. The dog may bring the larger one anyway because he has already been rewarded for this several times.

3 Repeat until you can place both objects next to one another in random sequence and the dog brings the right one.

Repeat steps 2 and 3 with the second largest and the smallest item.

 Now use all four objects. Show him the largest and the smallest. He will probably bring you the largest because he has already been rewarded for it.

 Next show him the third largest and the smallest object. This is the first check to see if he really understands the task, because up to now he has not received a reward for either of these objects.

When the dog consistently brings the right item in the sixth step, it is time to introduce the command for this task. This can be a verbal cue, (like "Bring Biggest"), or any desired start signal that will be simple for the dog to understand. Other tasks have demonstrated that he understands words—here he should concentrate on other things.

 Now present all possible combinations in different order and strengthen the command.

(continued)

9 Now comes the real test. Show the dog two identical objects of different sizes, other than those you have used for practice up to now.

Does he understand what you want him to do? If not, repeat the training steps with an another set of objects and then test him again.

🐾 Important

Make sure that the size of the objects are easily distinguishable. Don't expect the dog to make a decision that would be hard for a human to make because the size of the items are really too close to distinguish.

WHEN SHOULD I PROCEED TO THE NEXT STEP?

Good training really depends on how well you use the training steps. It is necessary for the dog to understand the task well before proceeding; but you shouldn't spend too much time on one training step while developing a behavior. Otherwise you waste valuable training time and, depending on the task, the dog will get too many rewards for intermediate steps, which could lead to misunderstandings.

90 % Rule

During training a good indicator that you can move on to the next step is when a behavior is successful 80 - 90 % of the time. This means repeating the same training step ten times. If the dog is successful nine times out of ten, you can proceed to the next step. However, repeating the same training step ten times is usually too boring for the trainer as well as the dog. Repeating five times is more practical; so 90% success rate would then be 4.5 times, which rounds out to 5 times. If a behavior is successful five out of five tries, it is time to go to the next step.

Traffic light training

We can combine the concept of traffic light training with the 90 % rule, which means:

If five repetitions are successful the traffic light is green, and you can go on to the next step. If only three or four repetitions out of five are successful, the light is yellow. You should practice this step a little more, and do five more repetitions. If only one or two repetitions are successful, the light is red and it is necessary to go back one step to continue your training.

SNAP

SNAP is an acronym you can use to help decide when it is time to proceed with the next training step.

The **"S"** stands for **"Success rate."** This is the 90 % rule. You can proceed with the next training step only when the success rate is high enough.

"N" stands for **"Necessary speed."** This means that the dog performs the behavior with a speed appropriate for him. This means the speed with which the task itself is performed, not the time the dog requires before he starts the behavior, (described below under prompt execution).

"A" stands for **"Accuracy."** Does the dog perform the exercise with the accuracy we want?

And finally **"P"** for **"Prompt execution."** The dog should react immediately with the appropriate behavior in the specific situation. If training has progressed to the point that a signal has been introduced, the dog should react immediately to it. If a signal has not yet been introduced, the surroundings themselves should provide the dog with sufficient information for him to react. For example, when you present him the rope, he should pull on it immediately, without waiting two or three seconds.

If one of these four criteria is not met, you should reconsider your training steps. "Prompt execution" and "necessary speed" usually provide the most accurate information. If delays occur, even though everything else is fulfilled, it may be that you have already worked too long or the dog is no longer certain what to do, even when the result still appears okay. For the trainer this means: Be attentive!

Rope Task

This exercise was once a research experiment for comparing the cognitive abilities of dogs with those of monkeys. The task was to get the animals to pull a rope out of a transparent box to get a reward. The challenge was to place a second rope in the box without a reward, so the animal had to choose.

Here are the arrangements for the two ropes:

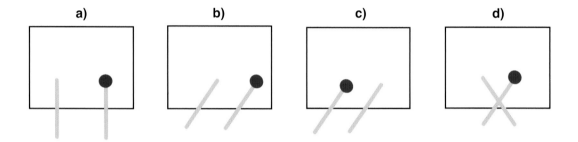

The monkeys (as well as the dogs) were capable of solving tasks a) and b). The dogs failed with tasks c) and d). Was this due to a lack of cognitive ability on the part of the dogs, or simply failure to make it clear to them what they were to do?

1 Practice with only one rope (one that is marked at the end with colored tape) and have the dog pull it out of the box. Position it at various angles. Reward the dog with a click and treat.

Now place a second, unmarked rope in the box as shown in arrangement a). Initially place the ropes as far apart as possible. When the dog picks the right one quite reliably, start moving the ropes closer together.

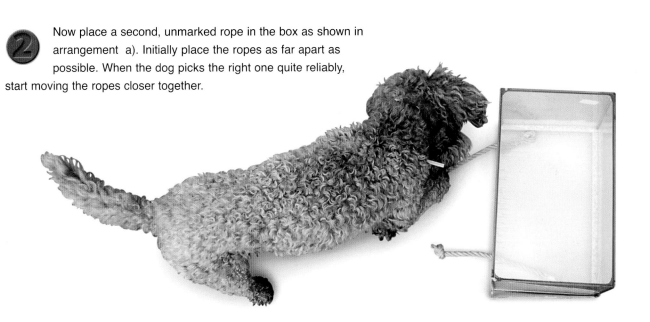

When the dog is consistently picking the right one, place a third unmarked rope in the box. We want to sharpen his vision. Continue to change the order until the dog picks the right rope every time.

(continued)

4 Now position the second rope as shown in arrangement b). Again start with two ropes positioned as far apart as possible and move them closer together little by little when the dog successfully picks the right one. To prevent the dog learning to just "pull the rope on the right," position the rope to be pulled randomly to the left and right of the other rope.

5 We now come to the point where the dogs failed in the original experiment (arrangement c). Add some intermediate steps here. Start with two ropes positioned fairly far apart. You can also use ropes of two different colors or two different materials to help the dog get the idea. When the exercise is successful with the ropes far apart, start moving them closer together. Then all other aids should be eliminated, of course.

6 In the last step position the ropes so that they cross over one another (as shown in arrangement d). Start with ropes of two different colors, but the colored tape should not always be on the same rope. When the dog no longer has any problem choosing the right one, start using two identical ropes.

🐾 Important

During the course of training, you should continuously change the "reward" rope. Otherwise the dog would only learn to pull out "his" rope, which would not be any problem for him with his sense of smell. But that is not the objective of this task.

We didn't differientiate the ropes by attaching a treat to one of them. Instead, we wrapped a piece of colored tape around one end. Since the dog gets the click and treat when he pulls it out, it is not necessary for the reward to be fastened to the rope itself. This could even distract the dog too much from the actual task, particularly with dogs who are really crazy about food. Naturally, it is hard for the dog to think under such circumstances.

Is my suspicion right, that this problem has more to do with the training method than the dog's cognitive ability? Does the dog really know to pull out the right rope, or simply "his" rope because he can differentiate between the two on the basis of the odor from touching the end of one of them? Are other factors involved?

Copy Dog

It can be very practical to teach your dog to mimic tricks or feats they see another dog doing. For a long time we thought dogs were incapable of doing this at all. However, anyone with more than one dog knows of situations where one dog has copied the behavior of another (usually things we would rather not have them do).

This is a good challenge for training, and the more concepts your dog has learned the more successful you will be.

For training you need another dog who can already perform a large number of tricks or feats. Your dog should already be able to do at least five simple things that the other dog can do.

1 Pick out a signal for "Copy." In addition to the verbal cue, you should also have a body signal, because the dog understands them better. Then have your "Demonstration dog" follow a command in the immediate vicinity, for example "Sit." Then give the "Copy" signal and then the command for "Sit" to your dog. Reward your dog and repeat this sequence a number of times.

← "Demonstration dog"

The blankets should always be identical.

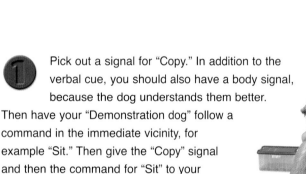

The **"Copy dog"** also gets the signal for "Sit" for better understanding

When you and your dog are familiar with the training sequence, select at least two more commands to have the dog perform in this manner: "Down" and "Roll over" for example. The demonstration dog performs first, you give your dog the "Copy" signal and then the appropriate command for the behavior the other dog has demonstrated. Repeat this in random order until it is no longer necessary to give the subsequent command following the "Copy" signal, because your dog already understands that he is supposed to do the same thing as the other dog. Be patient, this doesn't happen in a day. It is necessary for the dog to learn quite a bit to understand this concept.

Laios watches the other dog...

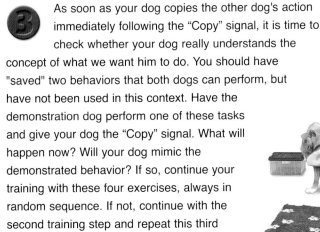

...and lies down without a signal.

 As soon as your dog copies the other dog's action immediately following the "Copy" signal, it is time to check whether your dog really understands the concept of what we want him to do. You should have "saved" two behaviors that both dogs can perform, but have not been used in this context. Have the demonstration dog perform one of these tasks and give your dog the "Copy" signal. What will happen now? Will your dog mimic the demonstrated behavior? If so, continue your training with these four exercises, always in random sequence. If not, continue with the second training step and repeat this third step later.   (continued)

★ ★ ★   Copy Dog   **129**

4 Now add the last task both dogs can perform. Your dog already has a pretty good idea of what you want him to do if he mimics this behavior. Repeat all five tasks to be copied several times.

5 Now comes the hard part! Have the demonstration dog perform an exercise your dog cannot yet do. This should be a relatively simple exercise, not one that requires a great deal of muscle or body coordination. Reward every attempt your dog makes to copy! This is a tremendous accomplishment for your dog. Repeat this exercise until it is really successful.

6 Continue to repeat the familiar exercises again and again. Have your dog copy a new task from time to time. Make sure that he is not given any help, other than what the other dog demonstrates.

Important

You need to make sure that your dog really understands the concept behind this exercise and you do not give him any unintentional signs which could lead to a "Clever Hans effect."

7 When your dog is successful in mimicking another dog, you can also use a different dog for demonstration. This way your dog can learn to copy tasks from any other dog. The only prerequisite is that the dogs get along well. This task requires quite a bit of brainwork from your dog. It won't be possible for him if he is stressed due to the presence of another dog he doesn't like.

★ ★ ★ Copy Dog **131**

Do What I Do

This exercise also consists of mimicking actions, however this time the dog is supposed to copy a human instead of another dog. This task is challenging for him, because now he is copying another species. This method was first used at the University of Budapest to teach a dog tasks as a helper for disabled humans.

As a prerequisite the dog should be able to perform at least six to eight different tasks. It would be ideal if he were also familiar with two or three other exercises to use for testing later.

1 Come up with a ritual for this exercise. The dog should watch you and then mimic what you show him. This should be practiced on something consistent, like on a certain blanket. This way you can always take it with you and use the same starting ritual at different locations.

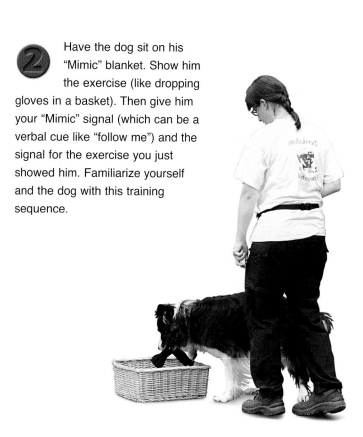

2 Have the dog sit on his "Mimic" blanket. Show him the exercise (like dropping gloves in a basket). Then give him your "Mimic" signal (which can be a verbal cue like "follow me") and the signal for the exercise you just showed him. Familiarize yourself and the dog with this training sequence.

3 As soon as the training sequence is clear for you and the dog, go through several exercises in random sequence with the dog. For example, lie down and tell the dog "Follow me" and then give him the signal for "Down." Turn around on your feet and hands and give the dog the signal for "Follow me" then the signal for "Turn around." Roll over on the floor and give the dog the signal "Follow me," then for "Roll over," etc. Do this until the dog no longer waits for the signal following the "mimic" signal and does the exercise immediately. Have patience. This requires a great deal of brainwork on the part of your dog. (continued)

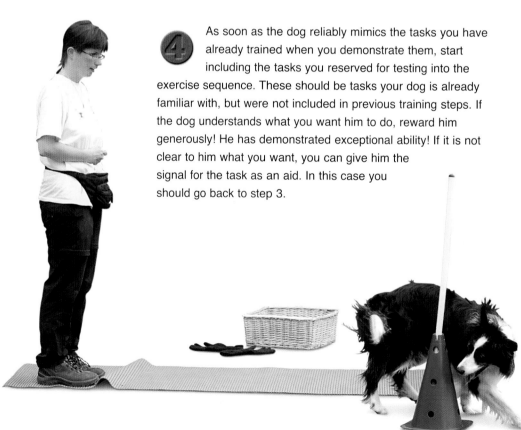

4. As soon as the dog reliably mimics the tasks you have already trained when you demonstrate them, start including the tasks you reserved for testing into the exercise sequence. These should be tasks your dog is already familiar with, but were not included in previous training steps. If the dog understands what you want him to do, reward him generously! He has demonstrated exceptional ability! If it is not clear to him what you want, you can give him the signal for the task as an aid. In this case you should go back to step 3.

5 If the dog has understood the test exercise, you can start showing him completely new things. At first, select things that don't require a great deal of body coordination or muscle. Did he understand the exercise? Congratulations! You have again proven the exceptional ability of yourself as a trainer as well as that of your dog.

6 Now practice things that the dog requires more time to learn. Crawling, for example, or standing up on his hind legs. For these tricks it is necessary for most dogs to first train their muscles for a while, so give him sufficient time.

7 Now you can also try tasks that are not typical for dogs. For example, what does you dog do when you open a cupboard door with your hand? Does the dog understand that the important thing is opening the door, not using his paw? He could pull on a piece of rope fastened to the door handle. If your dog has achieved this training level, he has come a long way toward understanding concepts and his accomplishment is remarkable!

Acknowledgements

It's important for me to thank my models for their exceptional work. The dogs' efforts and achievements were truly remarkable! Naturally this also applies for the humans! It's true, "The better the trainer, the smarter the dog" (Bob Bailey). The photos didn't just happen—in many cases it was necessary to practice a task for 6 months!

And I would also like to thank the dogs for their patience during the photography work, with lots of requests like: "Once more please." or "OK, that was pretty good, but you need to stay on the steps."

My thanks therefore to Michaela with Silas, Lisa with Nuja, Laios and Lovis, Britta with Luna, Ilona with Tommy, Gisela with Nelly, Jacqueline with Romeo and Shakespeare, Malu with Abba, Christiane with Liska, Susanne with Filouo, Dagmar with Sega, Pam with Haidée, Elfriede with Shogun, Steffie with Bessy, Jessica with Joule, Silke with Cara, Marina with Afra, Farid with Snoopy, Tina with Nele, Katja with Tofu, Josef and Corinna with Buka, Chiara with Holly and Delia with Jasou and Damon, Matz and Karli, and Andrea with Spike and Sina.

Thanks also to the photographers Brigitte and Dagmar, who took over for me when I was the one being photographed.

Thank you to Bernd for constructing the wonderful props. And to you as well as the other husbands and boyfriends who had to take a backseat to the dogs while your wives were training them so diligently.

My special thanks also to the scientists at the Universities in Budapest and Leipzig, whose work gave me so many ideas for this book. Perhaps you will also benefit from this later, when even better trainers provide the basis for establishing the cognitive abilities of dogs.

I would also like to thank Bob Bailey particularly, who taught me in his chicken camps that training is, in fact, a mechanical skill, which one can always continue to improve. You opened up new horizons for me, which I have now only just started to explore. It is truly fascinating how new worlds can open up! Thank you, because my life will certainly not be boring in the next few years!

Feedback

Did you notice anything particular when using the exercises presented in this book for your training? Where did you have difficulties, where did you have unexpected success? Have you worked out a creative task yourself or has your dog perhaps exhibited a new behavior on his own that you didn't intend or expect at all? I would be very pleased to hear your feedback, because I am curious to find out what your dog can do.

On my homepage at www.tierakademie.de I also offer a "smart dog forum" where you can register and exchange ideas, etc. with other trainers.

Please send your feedback to:

Tierakademie Scheuerhof
Viviane Theby
Scheuerhof
D-54516 Wittlich-Bombogen
GERMANY
scheuerhof@t-online.de

I am looking forward to hearing from you.

Front cover photo credits (montage) -- Shutterstock: Eric Isselée; Margo Harrison; Todd Taulman; Kitch Bain; Celso Diniz; m.p.imageart; Elenamiv

Back cover photo credits -- Shutterstock: Steven Pepple

The Models

Abba
Hovawart
2 years old

Afra
Pointer
6 years old

Bessy
German Hunt
Terrier Mix
5 years old

Cara
Labrador Retriever
4 years old

Damon
Lagotto
Romagnolo
4 years old

Filou
Berger de Pyrénées
2 years old

Holly
Lagotto
Romagnolo
2 years old

Joule
Australian Shepherd
2 years old

Haideé
French Bulldog
1 year old

Liska
Tervueren
6 years old

Lovis
Koiker Hondje
5 years old

Laios
Nova Scotia Duck
Tolling Retriever
2 years old

Luna
Small
Munsterland
9 years old

Nele
German Shepherd Mix
6 years old

Nelly
Golden
Retriever
3 years old

Nuja
Nova Scotia
Duck Tolling
Retriever
4 years old

Romeo & Shakespeare
Lagotto Romagnolo
4 years old
& 1 year
old

Sega
German
Shepherd Mix
5 years old

Seven
Australian
Shepherd
1 year old

Snoopy
Border Collie
1 year old

Tofu
Shetland Sheepdog
4 month old

Silas
Border Collie
12 years old

Sina
Old German
Shepherd
Tiger
3 years old

Spike
Border Collie
Mix
6 years old

Tommy
Mutt
6 years old

The "Smart Dog Diploma"

We have developed a "Smart Dog Diploma" at three levels (degrees of difficulty), which requires mastering various tasks from this book. The tasks are classified into various categories including "Target training," "Signal control," "Differentiation tasks," "Behavior chain" and, at level 3, "Understanding concepts."

(More information on the test is available at www.tierakademie.de.)

In the category "Target training" it is necessary for the dog to demonstrate that he can touch a target and follow it, and perform a task trained using a target.

In the category "Signal control" the dog has to demonstrate his understanding of four commands using a verbal cue. This can be four actions such as "Sit," "Down," "Bow" and "Wave," or the dog can identify four different objects when given the word for them.

In the category "Differentiation tasks" the dog should be able to perform two of the following tasks reliably: "Find a certain smell," "Find a certain color," or "Show a certain shape," and in each case he must choose from four possibilities.

In the category "Behavior chain" the dog must demonstrate a chain consisting of five parts (which may be associated with one another). He should perform this chain on signal. The table below lists other items to be tested.

These are – as already mentioned – very demanding tasks. But it is fun to find out what your dog can do. And, of course, it continues to improve your communication.

Requirements for Levels 1 - 3

	Target training	Signal control	Differentiation tasks	Behavior chain	Concepts
Level 1	• Touch a target • Follow a target • Train a task using a target	• An object as signal • Perform 4 commands on verbal cue or • Show 4 objects when named	Two of the following tasks: • Find a smell • Find a shape • Find a color from a selection of four choices	Perform a behavior chain consisting of 5 parts, (which maybe associated with one another), on signal	Not required for Level 1

	Target training	Signal control	Differentiation tasks	Behavior chain	Concepts
Level 2	• Stationed on target with distraction • On two targets simultaneously	• 7 commands on verbal cue • Continue performing one command until stopped • 4 commands with an object or • Command consisting of two parts	One of the following exercises: • Find the same • Vision test • Counting dog • Reading dog • Bring the same and • Right/left or • Higher/lower	• Perform a behavior chain consisting of 7 parts (which may be associated with one another), on signal • Perform a behavior chain consisting of 5 parts, which are not all associated with one another	Not required for Level 2
Level 3	• Stationed on target and then shape something • On three targets simultaneously	• Command as secondary reinforcer and • Figure eight or circle or • Signal and target similar	• Command consisting of 3 parts	• Memorize sequence consisting of 3 behaviors not associated with one another in any manner	Perform one of the following tasks: • Be creative • Concept of middle • Which is biggest? • Rope task • Copy dog • Do what I do

SMART DOG
UNIVERSITY

_____
Dog's Name

_____
Date

SMART DOG U

GLOSSARY

capturing: A training approach that reinforces a behavior that a dog performs spontaneously by marking the behavior and rewarding it

chaining: linking several behaviors together in a chain (a specific sequence). When the last behavior is taught first, this is called *back chaining*.

clicker training: A form of training based on operant conditioning in which the dog learns to associate a marker (in this case, the sound of the click) with a reward

ethogram: a description of a animal's normal behavior. The behaviors are usually listed with precise definitions, and then grouped into categories

cue: a word or action used to prompt a behavior

latency: Response time

luring: A training approach in which a dog is enticed to perform an action with a reward, usually a treat or toy

mark: The act of signaling to a dog to denote a very specific action or behavior

marker: A signal, usually auditory but sometimes visual or tactile, that indicates, or marks, a very specific action or behavior

modeling: A training approach that involves a person physically positioning or moving a dog to perform an action that the dog will eventually perform on his own

operant conditioning: A form of learning in which the dog learns to associate a marker with a reward

positive reinforcement: adding something the dog wants in order to increase the likelihood that the behavior will occur again

primary reinforcer: A reward that the dog values by nature, like food

punishment: anything that will decrease the likelihood of a behavior occurring again

reinforcer: *See* reward

reward: Something that a dog gets as a result of behaving in a certain way. Rewards are used extensively in positive training to motivate learning and occasionally later to reinforce established behaviors

secondary reinforcer: A reward that has acquired value for the learner by being associated with a primary reinforcer

shaping: A training approach in which a desired behavior is broken down into tiny increments

signal: a cue that prompts a behavior. Signals can include hand signals, body motions, or even objects

targeting: A training approach that teaches a dog to touch a specific object to earn a reward (a treat at first, then verbal rewards punctuated by occasional treats)

RESOURCES

Clubs and Registries

American Kennel Club (AKC)
5580 Centerview Drive
Raleigh, NC 27606
Telephone: (919) 233-9767
Fax: (919) 233-3627
E-mail: info@akc.org
www.akc.org

American Mixed Breed Obedience Registration (AMBOR)
PO Box 223
Anoka, MN 55303
E-mail: ambor@ambor.us
www.ambor.us

North American Mixed Breed Registry (NAMBR)
RR#2 - 8649 Appleby Line
Campbellville, Ontario
Canada L0P 1B0
E-mail: info@nambr.ca
www.nambr.ca

United Kennel Club (UKC)
100 E. Kilgore Road
Kalamazoo, MI 49002-5584
Telephone: (269) 343-9020
Fax: (269) 343-7037
E-mail: pbickell@ukcdogs.com
www.ukcdogs.com

Training and Behavior Resources

Animal Behavior Society (ABS)
Certified Applied Animal Behaviorist
Directory:
www.animalbehavior.org/ABSAppliedBehavior/caab-directory

Association of Pet Dog Trainers (APDT)
150 Executive Center Drive Box 35
Greenville, SC 29615
Telephone: (800) PET-DOGS
Fax: (864) 331-0767
E-mail: information@apdt.com
www.apdt.com

Further Reading

The following books offer valuable basic knowledge and fascinating stories about the method of working with dogs described in this book:

Bailey, Bob: *The Fundamentals of Animal Training by Bob Bailey.* DVD. Dog Sports Video, Las Vegas, 2006.

Csányi, Vilmos: *If Dogs Could Talk: Exploring the Canine Mind.* North Point Press, New York, 2005.

Pryor, Karen: *Getting Started: Clicker Training for Dogs.* Sunshine Books, Weston (MA), 4 edition 2005

Pryor, Karen: *Lads before the wind – Diary of a Dolphin Trainer.* Sunshine Books, Weston (MA), 2004.

Ramirez, Ken: *Animal Training. Successful animal management through positive reinforcement.* Shed Aquarium Society, Chicago (IL), 1999.

Topal, J.; Byrne, R. W,; Miklosi, A. und Csanyi, V.: »Reproducing human actions and action sequences: ›Do as I do‹ in a dog«, in: *Anim. Cogn.* 9 (2006), S. 355 - 367.

Yin, Dr. Sophia: *How to Behave So Your Dog Behaves.* TFH Publications, New Jersey, 2004.

Solution to question on Page 61:

The dog looks much happier when he comes from the "Bow" blanket.

"Bow" blanket

"Come" blanket

NATURAL with added VITAMINS

Nutri Dent®

Promotes Optimal Dental Health!

Visit nylabone.com
Join Club NYLA!
get coupons & product information

360° Design
Cleaning Action!™

USA MADE

Dogs Love 'em!™

AVAILABLE IN MULTIPLE SIZES AND FLAVORS.

Nylabone®

Trusted for Over 50 Years

A275

Our Mission with Nutri Dent® is to promote optimal dental health for dogs through a trusted, natural, delicious chew that provides effective cleaning action... GUARANTEED to make your dog go wild with anticipation and happiness!!!

Nylabone Products • P.O. Box 427, Neptune, NJ 07754-0427 • 1-800-631-2188 • Fax: 732-988-5466
www.nylabone.com • info@nylabone.com • For more information contact your sales representative or contact us at sales@tfh.com